6-9-66

HOW CAPITALISM CAN SUCCEED

a primer of economic choices for people who want to be both **prosperous and free** /

STACKPOLE BOOKS

HOW CAPITALISM CAN SUCCEED

Spencer D. Pollard, Ph.D.
Professor of Economics
University of Southern California

HOW CAPITALISM CAN SUCCEED

THE STACKPOLE COMPANY
Cameron and Kelker Streets
Harrisburg, Pa. 17105

Library of Congress
catalogue card number
66-12780

Printed in the U.S.A.

10

Contents

Part II. Hurdles on the Path to Prosperity

Part III. The Struggle for the World

CHAPTER 1

Prosperity and Freedom

Many people will react to the title of this book by saying, "But capitalism has already succeeded!" And so it has in parts of the world—in northern Europe, in most of North America, in Hawaii, Australia, New Zealand, and Japan—to name the larger areas. Yet most of the world's people still live in poverty under dictatorships of right or left, far from the combination of prosperity and freedom for all which it is the ideal of capitalism to create.

Even in the successful capitalistic nations, as their economic systems have grown more complex, there has arisen the danger that their own people, confused and divided by political slogans of right and left, will throw away their success by ill-advised actions for lack of understanding of what successful capitalism is and what it requires of them.

The purpose of this book is to give the citizens of the free economies, whether executives, housewives, scientists, workers, students, or politicians, who have had no formal training in economics the opportunity to understand the economic system of which they are a part and for whose preservation and growth they are responsible. Such understanding will not be entirely an act of unselfish public service, since the citizens' own incomes and their own freedoms depend as much upon the way the economy goes as upon their own individual efforts.

The goal of simplicity in understanding capitalism—and, as we shall stress, understanding what *complete* capitalism is—can be reached by dividing the system into its major parts and looking at them one by one. There are five of these parts which we shall call the procedures, or components, of capitalism.

1. Competition
2. Innovation
3. Full employment
4. Countervailing power
5. Stimulation

By competition we mean preparing people during about the first third of their lives to be fit for freedom, to be qualified to be let alone to work out their own economic destinies under the law of supply and demand.

By innovation we mean the creation of co-operating groups of people including religious leaders and philosophers, scientists, inventors, investors, employees, sellers, and consumers to keep a continual flow of new things coming into human hands, to be used wisely and well.

By full employment, we mean a procedure for insuring that there will be no depressions. This requires us to see the circulation of money in the whole economy as though it were a hydraulic system. When leakages from the system in the form of savings, taxes, and purchases abroad are properly balanced by injections into the system in the form of private investment, government spending, and sales abroad, then the system will be steady. The full employment procedure consists of means of influencing these leakages and injections to prevent depression.

The component of countervailing power requires the distribution of economic power among organized groups representing all elements of the population including business, labor, agriculture, science, education, the old, the poor, the unemployed, the government, etc. Its purpose is to end dictatorial forms of government which result when all power is given to any one group.

Stimulation needs to be listed as a component of a free economy, since history teaches us that eras of prosperity in free nations have always been associated with certain underlying beliefs about the duties and goals of individuals in life. A very prominent system of such beliefs is called the Protestant Ethic, but there are similar "prosperity ethics" to be found in other religions and philosophies.

When a free economy has these five procedures built and operating, it may fairly be called a "complete" capitalism. However, we all recognize that any piece of equipment, including a whole economy, has certain operating problems which need to be handled properly. At this moment in history the most important ones facing capitalism, apart from sheer physical security against its enemies, are population, automation, inflation, and debt, and we intend to discuss each of them.

Finally we must face the enemy itself and consider ideas opposing an economy of choice. These are the ideologies of determinism which say that man's economic fate is sealed by natural or human facts or by inevitable chains of events which, once set in motion, must grind on to foreseeable but unavoidable ends—fixed dances of life and death. This is where Marxism belongs.

What the chances of these competing ideologies are in the present battle for the world will be the subject of our concluding chapter.

Before plunging into our main discussion, let us be sure, when we set our goal as a combination of freedom and prosperity, that we know what we mean by these two potent words.

As for "freedom," we do not intend to disagree with the philosopher who tells us that no man is free. We are all limited to some extent by our heredity and environment, friends and enemies, private compulsions, and spendable incomes. Freedom under capitalism means the absence of restraint by tyrannical authority over the individual in making specific economic decisions.

While economists have not yet drawn up a complete list of such freedoms, such a list would certainly include freedom of the individual to choose these for himself:

1. Schools, colleges, and universities
2. Jobs and professions
3. Employers
4. Enterprises to engage in
5. Investments
6. Goods and services
7. Merchants
8. Group associations

9. Beliefs and expression
10. Leisure activities
11. Residence and travel
12. Mate and number of offspring

In any society we are likely to construct, there will be limitations imposed upon the extremes of the spectrum of choice in all such decisions, but there is no mistaking the very wide latitude allowed the individual in these matters under successful capitalism as compared with any other form of society past or present. The planned societies of right or left force the individual to accept governmental decisions in all or nearly all of these areas.

By "prosperity" we shall not mean simply a greedy accumulation of material things by people who do not care for non-material values. On the contrary, an economy cannot be called prosperous until it supplies the means of satisfying a well-balanced variety of human necessities and luxuries including spiritual, artistic, intellectual, and emotional wants in addition to material ones.

It may be helpful to our thinking to divide the fruits of prosperity into ten kinds. The first five are the basic necessities—food, clothing, housing, rudimentary education, and medical care. There will be little dispute about these. In addition to being necessary to life, these basic five are also insufficient for a good life. They are to be found in well-run prisons from which it is the ambition of nearly every inmate to escape.

What makes life worth living if we have the basic five is an additional set of goods and services which we call the extra five:

1. *Good surroundings*—pure air, water, and food, clean streets, lovely parks, uncluttered highways, etc.
2. *Recreation*—time and facilities for physical, mental, and emotional recreation; scientific, artistic, and creative recreation as well as playful and romantic recreation; and active recreation as participants in addition to spectator recreation.
3. *Good human relations*—within the family, the social group, the nation, and the world.
4. *Work in line with our developed talents.* There is almost universal testimony that proper work increases the satisfaction of living. (See also the chapter on Automation.)
5. *Freedoms*—of all the kinds we have listed above.

Some may question the logic of including freedoms in our definition of prosperity, since we have already given them separate standing in the phrase "prosperity and freedom." The advantage of making freedoms one of the ten kinds of goods and services which a successful economy must supply is that the list then is complete. It is prosperous man's shopping list. He takes the list to the supermarket which we call our economic system, and he buys different quantities of each kind of good or service according to his philosophy of life.

Some may object to including freedoms and good human relations as kinds of "goods and services." The reason for including them, apart from the values they add to living, is that they really are produced by directing men, money, equipment, and management to that end in the same sense that automobiles are produced. The production of freedoms requires constitutions, congresses, courts, police, attorneys, clerks, schools, books, organizations, and all their usual gear. The production of good human relations, over and above their natural level, which does not seem to be high, requires educators, counselors, conciliators, referees, contracts, pacts, treaties, and all the personnel to man them.

In sum, we shall call capitalism complete when it has all five of its necessary components and when it devotes them to the production of all ten kinds of goods and services. In addition, we shall call it successful when it also handles its major operating problems well and secures itself against its deterministic enemies.

Part I

The Make-Up of Complete Capitalism

CHAPTER **2**

Becoming Economically Sophisticated Citizens: the element of competition

Classical economics, beginning with Adam Smith's *Wealth of Nations* (1776) and culminating in Alfred Marshall's *Principles of Economics* (1890), recognized that if man is to combine freedom and prosperity he will have to evolve a new personality. This new person is called Economic Man.

Economic Man is different from any major type of human personality of the past. He is not Rousseau's natural man, since the "noble savage" would require a great deal of civilization to become an economic man. Nor could he be the ascetic man of the Middle Ages, denying himself earthly pleasures in hope of heaven. And not the Spartan warrior, nor the Confucian gentleman studying his ancient texts, nor the Southern gentleman contemplating his mid-morning julep. And certainly not the slave-rowers of

Cleopatra's barge or the feudal peasant fearing his lord. Nor would he be the greedy, short-sighted, narrow-minded materialist that some romanticists have mistakenly supposed the classical economists to mean by the term "economic man."

The Creation of Economic Man

Adam Smith said that the recipe for combining prosperity and freedom was simple. It had only three ingredients:

1. Individual competition
2. Co-operation through specialization
3. Little government activity in economic life

Smith wanted each individual to be self-reliant and not to depend upon combinations with others to achieve special gains or subsidies for himself. He recognized that productivity depends upon working with others; but the proper formula for this, he said, was for each person to do the particular part of the work at which he was best, and then pass the unfinished product on to the next specialist. Government, which had played so large a part in economic affairs throughout history, was to confine itself to the mails, the roads, and the armed forces. Competition, in short, was to be "pure," that is, free of monopolistic devices, private or public.

To Smith's recipe there was added by later classical economists the ideal of "perfect" competition, that is, a condition to be attained by making men and women, at least in their economic activities, rational, knowing, and mobile. By rationality, the Classicals meant that people should pursue their own "enlightened self-interest," not with short-sighted greed at one extreme or with impulsive destructiveness at the other, but with reasoned assessments and reassessments of their own best good in the long run. By knowledge, the Classicals meant that people should have enough education and current information to know where their best opportunities are to be found. And by mobility, they meant that people should be able to move from here to there, geographically and socially, to take advantage of their best opportunities. There was to be no chaining of individuals by caste or fealties to inferior walks of life.

To this portrait, Alfred Marshall, the great systematizer of classical economics, added two other characteristics—skill and health. It is often said that the classical economists were in favor of complete laissez-faire in economic matters, but this was true only after the point where Economic Man had been created. They recognized the duty of the State in the act of his creation. Like the other classical economists, Marshall was no advocate of a sink-or-swim philosophy of human life, and it is worth anyone's while to listen to what he was saying in the early years of the twentieth century about the skill and health of the working classes.

> We have then to strive to keep mechanical progress in full swing: and to diminish the supply of labor incapable of any but unskilled work, in order that the average income of the country may rise faster even than in the past, and the share of it got by each unskilled laborer may rise faster still. To that end we need to move in the same direction as in recent years, but more strenuously. Education must be made more thorough. The schoolmaster must learn that his main duty is not to impart knowledge, for a few shillings will buy more printed knowledge than a man's brain can hold. It is to educate character, faculties and activities; so that the children even of those parents who are not thoughtful themselves, may have a better chance of being trained up to become thoughtful parents of the next generation. To this end public money must flow freely. And it must flow freely

> to provide fresh air and space for wholesome play for the children in all working class quarters.
>
> Thus the State seems to be required to contribute generously and even lavishly to that side of the well-being of the poorer working class which they cannot easily provide for themselves: and at the same time to insist that the inside of the houses be kept clean, and fit for those who will be needed in after years to act as strong and responsible citizens. The compulsory standard of cubic feet of air per head needs to be raised steadily though not violently: and this combined with a regulation that no row of high buildings be erected without adequate free space in front and behind, will hasten the movement, already in progress, of the working classes from the central districts of large towns, to places in which freer playroom is possible. Meanwhile public aid and control in medical and sanitary matters will work in another direction to lessen the weight that has hitherto pressed on the children of the poorer classes.
>
> The children of unskilled workers need to be made capable of earning the wages of skilled work: and the children of skilled workers need by similar means to be made capable of doing still more responsible work.[1]

In sum, we find that by the early years of the twentieth century the classical economists had built up a portrait of Economic Man as a person motivated to economic progress, self-reliant but willing to co-operate with others through minute division of labor, and as a rational, knowledgeable, and mobile man or woman possessed of as much health and skill as can be built into him or her.

In view of the criticisms so often made of the very idea of Economic Man, it is worth noting that his portrait was created by men who were themselves educated and humane in very high degree. Adam Smith was Professor of Moral Philosophy at the Universities of Edinburgh and Glasgow.

In his *Theory of Moral Sentiments,* which should be read along with the *Wealth of Nations,* he explained his ideal of human conduct as based upon humane generosity and warmth of spirit. Smith was himself a man of wide culture, writing about astronomy, literature, and the fine arts as well as politics and economics. John Stuart Mill, the second great classical economist, is famous for his account of his own severely intellectual upbringing, for his essay, *On Liberty,* and for his *Principles of Political Economy with Some of Their Applications to Social Philosophy*. And Alfred Marshall, the third of the great trio of English classical economists, was a professor at Cambridge University, a brilliant teacher and a gentle and generous person, qualities which show through clearly in his reflections on life in his *Principles of Economics*. These were all gentle intellectuals, and contrary to their critics, Scrooge was not their ideal man. What they sought to do was to tell man what he had to become in order to be both free and prosperous.

Obeying the Law of Supply and Demand

If men are economic men, then, said the classical economists, the law of supply and demand will regulate their affairs quite satisfactorily without the necessity of government interference on the one hand or the prospect of anarchy on the other.

In its most general form, the law of supply and demand says that, in a world composed of the economic men and women we have been describing, changes within the economic system will be self-dampening, so that new positions of equilibrium will dependably arise. Therefore, we need not fear that economic freedom will result in any flying off the economic handle into disastrous or revolutionary situations.

Put more technically, the law says that taking the basic

variables of demand, price, and supply, in an initial position of equilibrium, any change in one of these variables will set up changes in the other two which will tend to slow and stop the original changes, until a new equilibrium is reached—perhaps at a different level of the variables, but nevertheless an equilibrium.

To take an example, suppose there is an increase in the demand for television sets. (By demand, economists mean effective demand, that is, the desire for the product plus the ability and willingness to pay for it.) As demand increases, merchants find it profitable to charge higher prices for their sets, and this effect tends to slow down the increase in demand, as some would-be purchasers find the new prices too steep for their liking. The increase in price, in turn, tends to encourage manufacturers to make more sets, and this in itself tends to dampen the increase in price. So finally a new equilibrium is reached at prices which keep demand and supply balanced.

To take another example, starting from the supply side, let us suppose that the supply of automobiles increases. The law of supply and demand says that the price of automobiles will consequently fall, and this fall will discourage some manufacturers from continuing the high output. The fall of price will also make it easier for consumers to buy automobiles, and the resultant increase in demand will take up the increase of supply, thus restoring equilibrium to the automobile situation.

Economists have shown by building geometric models that the tendency of markets undergoing changes to restore themselves to a condition of equilibrium will prevail even where there is a high concentration of production in a few firms, a condition increasingly prevalent under modern capitalism. This condition, known technically as oligopoly (meaning a situation where there are few sellers, a term parallel to oligarchy in political science), results, according to the mathematical models, in somewhat higher prices and lower output than would exist if there were more competitors, but these disadvantages may be offset by greater technical progress in the larger firms. What is important for the feasibility of capitalism is that the tendency to equilibrium has been shown to be present even in oligopolistic situations.

According to the classical law of supply and demand, therefore, all parts of the capitalist system show dominant tendencies to re-equilibrate themselves after disturbances, and do not need the heavy hand of government to set them right—assuming, of course, that the participants are classical economic men. When we are dealing with departures from this ideal—immobile farmers, or helpless children or unskilled unemployed, or the ill, the aged, and the criminally inclined, then the law of supply and demand will not work well and social action will need to be taken.

The classical economists also thought that the law of supply and demand operated for the economic system as a whole as well as for individual goods and services. In general, they said, if the law is left free to operate, all the things that there is a demand for will be supplied in the proper relative amounts, and the totality of things produced will be sold. This is called Say's Law of Markets, or simply Say's Law, after Jean-Baptiste Say (1767-1832), the first professor of economics in France. Say's Law was especially heartening because it seemed to prove that there can be no depressions under capitalism as long as fully competitive conditions prevail.

The Pessimists: Malthus, Ricardo, and Darwin

In creating their image of Economic Man, the classical economists expressed a degree of optimism about humanity which was unprecedented in man's thought about himself. One can imagine the astonishment on the faces of Plato, Aristotle, Aquinas, and Machiavelli, had they been told in all seriousness that ordinary human beings could become economic men and women possessing the characteristics we have mentioned and could thereupon be left free for the rest of their lives to make their own transactions with one another.

This classical optimism did not go unchallenged in the nineteenth century. The intellectual history of that century was marked by a tremendous struggle between the optimism of the classical economists about man's inherent abilities and the theories of a trio of powerful pessimists—Malthus, Ricardo, and Darwin.

Near the beginning of the century, Malthus issued his Iron Law of Population, saying in his famous *Essay*: "Population has this constant tendency to increase beyond the means of subsistence," and if we realize this, he continued: "We shall be compelled to acknowledge that the poverty and misery which prevail among the lower classes of society are absolutely irremediable."[2]

Ricardo picked up Malthus' views on population, added some observations on the scarcity of land and its control by a few landowners, and produced his Iron Law of Wages. This said that no matter how much economic progress was made, ordinary people would not share in it. They would always breed up to the point where competition for employment would keep their wages down to a bare subsistence level, and the fruits of economic progress would go entirely to the landlords.

Darwin's voice then chimed in with his Iron Law of Tooth and Claw. He was in the act of reading Malthus "for amusement," he tells us in his autobiography, when it suddenly occurred to him that Malthus' Law was applicable to all life on earth. Thus, Darwin concluded, in the last sentence of *The Origin of Species*: "From the war of nature, from famine and death, the most exalted object which we are capable of conceiving, namely the production of the higher animals, directly follows."

No wonder economics was known as "the dismal science"!

The Victory of Optimism

Malthus was the first of the trio of pessimists to soften the iron in his law. In his last book, *The Principles of Political Economy,* published in 1820, twenty-two years after his famous *Essay,* he finally agreed that working people have a choice about population. He wrote:

> From high real wages, or the power of commanding a larger portion of the necessities of life, two very different results may follow; one that of a rapid increase in population, in which case the high wages are chiefly spent in the maintenance of large and frequent families; and the other that of a decided improvement in the modes of subsistence, and the conveniences and comforts enjoyed, without a proportionate acceleration in the rate of increase.[3]

Which of these two possibilities, overbreeding or restraint, will actually occur, depends, says Malthus, on the outlook of the people. They will not overbreed if they are the sort who "look before and after and who consequently cannot acquiesce patiently in the thought of depriving themselves and their children of the means of being respectable, virtuous, and happy."[4]

And, Malthus continues, the most efficient causes of such a favorable attitude are civil and political liberty and education. He writes:

> Of all the causes which tend to generate prudential habits among the lower classes of society, the most es-

> sential is unquestionably civil liberty. No people can be much accustomed to form plans for the future who do not feel assured that their industrious exertions, while fair and honourable, will be allowed to have free scope; and that the property which they either possess, or may acquire, will be secured to them by a known code of just laws impartially administered. But it has been found by experience that civil liberty cannot be permanently secured without political liberty. Consequently, political liberty becomes almost equally essential; and in addition to its being necessary in this point of view, its obvious tendency to teach the lower classes of society to respect themselves by obliging the higher classes to respect them, must contribute greatly to aid all the good effects of civil liberty.
>
> With regard to education, it might certainly be made general, under a bad form of government, and might be very deficient under one in other respects good; but it must be allowed that the chances, both with regard to its quality and its prevalence, are greatly in favour of the latter. Education alone could do little against insecurity of property; but it would powerfully assist all the favourable consequences to be expected from civil and political liberty, which could not indeed be considered as complete without it.[5]

Thus Malthus finally joined the classical economists in saying that if human beings could achieve certain advantages and attitudes, they would not always breed themselves into poverty, and poverty would not always be irremediable. Malthus did not say, nor did any of the classical economists, that all men would make the right choices, but he did specify the particular choices which would have to be made to prevent excessive population.

Darwin also came over belatedly to the classical view. In his *Descent of Man,* he confessed that he had been disturbed by the awful implications for human society drawn from the *Origin of Species* published twelve years earlier. To clarify his views, he then gave his own theory of human development. Human progress, he wrote, depends upon the pursuit of a goal—the general good.

> The term general good may be defined as the rearing of the greatest number of individuals in full vigor and health with all their faculties perfect under the conditions to which they are subjected.[6]

What is the method of progress toward this goal? In Darwin's words:

> With highly civilized nations, continued progress depends in a subordinate degree on natural selection, for such nations do not supplant and exterminate one another as do savage tribes. . . . The more efficient causes of progress seem to consist of a good education during youth while the brain is impressible, and of a high standard of excellence inculcated by the ablest and best men, embodied in the laws, customs and traditions of the nation, and enforced by public opinion.[7]

As for the kinds of men who contribute to this education and excellence, Darwin says:

> Great lawgivers, the founders of beneficent religions, great philosophers and discoverers in science aid the progress of mankind in a far higher degree by their works than by leaving a numerous progeny.[8]

Therefore, Darwin concludes,

> Obscure as is the problem of the advance of civilization, we can at least see that the nation which produced, during a lengthened period, the greatest number of highly intellectual, energetic, brave, patriotic and benevolent men, would generally prevail over less favoured nations.[9]

If we then ask, as we must in dealing with any theory of evolution, how societies with such a large number of devoted people managed to come successfully through the earlier periods of history, when tribes did exterminate one another on the basis of natural selection, Darwin's answer is this:

> When two tribes of primeval man, living in the same country, came into competition, if (other circumstances being equal), the one tribe included a great number of courageous, sympathetic and faithful members, who were always ready to warn each other of danger, to aid and defend each other, this tribe would succeed better and conquer the other.[10]

Given the likelihood of this outcome, we must then ask why Darwin supposes that, within each tribe, the number of devoted people could increase, since those people by their very unselfishness and devotion were likely to expose themselves to more danger, and suffer earlier death, and leave fewer children, than the more selfish.

Darwin's answer is that devoted people propagate their own kind of personalities, not through their physical children, but through their ethical and intellectual children, that is, through those who imitate the actions of the devoted ones. The disciples that a devoted person can create, even in a short lifetime, are a much larger number, he says, than the children that a selfish man can leave behind, however long he lives.[11]

Thus Darwin, too, was won over to the possibility of human progress, so much so that he was willing, just as the classical economists were, to write down the choices men had to make to bring it about.

Ricardo alone, of the three, maintained his absolute pessimism. Perhaps there are excuses for him. He died when he was only fifty-one. He was preoccupied with the fortune he made in the stock market. His theory was based on rigidly logical deductions from narrow assumptions about scarce land and great landowners, while, beyond the purview of those assumptions, in new lands with new institutions, economic progress was being made which benefited the working classes. Even in old England, the workers were making progress to belie Ricardo's dismal prophecies. Nevertheless, his rigid reasoning and gloomy outlook lay ready when Marx came along, and Marx based his view of capitalism partly upon Ricardo's theories.

Thus the great battle of the nineteenth century between those who were optimistic about man's capabilities and those who were pessimistic about them was won substantially, though not totally, and at least temporarily, by the optimists.

Among the fruits of victory were new characteristics added to the picture of Economic Man. There was Malthus' view that such a man would rationally control his numbers if he had *hope, respect, civil liberty,* and *education.*

And there was Darwin's view that those groups of individuals would survive whose members had feelings of solidarity with one another rather than alienation and enough people sufficiently unselfish to devote themselves to the professions of science, teaching, religion, and statesmanship, even at material sacrifice to themselves.

Freud and Economic Rationality

It might have been expected that the image of Classical Economic Man as a practical, rational being would have been cracked or even broken by recent upheavals in psychological theory. Freud's picture of man's hot, volcanic subconscious, and Jung's emphasis upon the dominance of ancient myths and symbols seemed to say that man's mind was in chains, the chains of mishaps in his own childhood and in the childhood of his race.

But the classical economists had already insulated their Man against such an effect by their invention of a technique of rationality called "marginalism." They did not ask or expect that man should get up every morning and assure himself that his whole outlook on life was rational. Even the most devoted philosophers have not been willing to say that they could achieve that.

Under the doctrine of marginalism, rationality is a far less exacting task. Rationality in the consumer means that he is expected to examine consciously and regularly the amount of satisfaction he is getting out of the last dollar he is spending on each type of good and service he buys. If upon reflection he concludes that the last dollar he is spending on, say, automobile transportation, is being less helpful to him than the last dollar he is spending on education, then he should shift dollars from one to the other until the satisfaction he gets from the last dollar spent on each is the same. By applying this principle to his whole budget, he can achieve a maximum of satisfaction from it. That will occur at the point where no shift of dollars at the margins of expenditure would add to his total "utility" (the economists' word for satisfaction).

For the businessman, marginalism means spending his business money on labor, machinery, land, and management so that the net return from the last dollar spent on each is the same. If it is not, then his net return could be increased by shifting expenditure from one item to another. The same principle would apply to the businessman's expenditures upon the "mix" of different products and services he supplies to others.

For the worker (including executives), the practice of marginalism involves weighing the satisfactions and dissatisfactions of the last hours he spends on different kinds of work and different kinds of leisure in relation to the rewards from them, with a view to shifting time from one to another to keep the amounts of net satisfaction substantially equal.

Thus the doctrine of marginalism permitted the classical economists to be satisfied that a person is economically rational if he frequently reconsiders the direction of his energies and his purchasing power with a view to his greater satisfaction, in whatever way that satisfaction may be determined. This is a doctrine which begs many questions, but by it the classical economists protected their ideas, wisely or unwisely, from controversies in psychology and psychiatry.

Summary

The task economists have set themselves is to blueprint a new advance in human evolution—an advance to a stage where man can be both prosperous and free. The first component of this new era, or, to put it in another way, the first procedure that needs to be set up to achieve it, is a system of competition between individuals in an overall co-operative framework of a minute division of labor. To make this system work, individuals must be made into economic men and women.

The first accomplishment of the classical economists was to describe Economic Man as a person who is *self-reliant, motivated* to economic progress, *rational, knowledgeable, mobile, healthy,* and *skilled.* Malthus added the need to establish conditions under which man would control his numbers through having *hope, self-respect, civil liberty,* and *education.* Darwin spoke of the need for a degree of *solidarity* and *devotion* to assist the survival of the group in which the individual lives and works and seeks protection from enemies.

Unfortunately, men and women are not like this—or not sufficiently like it—as they come from the hand of the Creator, and the classical economists recognized that much time, energy, and money would have to be invested in people by their families, their institutions, and their governments to make them fit to be both free and prosperous. For those who achieve these characteristics, the great prize is that they may depend upon their own decisions and the decisions of other free men and women under the law of supply and demand to secure their prosperity without the necessity of dictatorship at one extreme or the fear of anarchy at the other.

CHAPTER 3

Producing Better Products: the element of innovation

The second element in complete capitalism is a procedure of innovation. This idea came into economic theory through the work of Joseph A. Schumpeter (1883-1950). Schumpeter's career included several false starts. He studied at the University of Vienna to become a lawyer, but gave up the law for economics. In 1919 he accepted the post of finance minister of Austria, and was forced to resign after only seven months because he could not control that nation's postwar inflation. In 1922 he became president of a small bank. It collapsed in 1924. Thereafter he taught economics at Bonn until 1932, when he came to teach at Harvard. His major works are *The Theory of Economic Development, Business Cycles, A History of Economic*

Analysis, and the book which is most useful to the layman, *Capitalism, Socialism and Democracy.*

Those of us who were his graduate students remember him as a man of great cultural enthusiasms, widely read in many languages, eager in his search for signs of new ideas in his students. His mind was so volatile that what he said in his lectures often astonished him with its significance, and he would sit down at once and make a note of it. (Surely there have been very few professors who took notes on their own lectures!)

The Meaning of Innovation

Schumpeter felt that the classical economists' prescription for competition did not provide for economic growth. They mentioned the matter frequently, but they seemed to suppose that it was a natural process, that the economy grows like a tree, and that the individuals whose acts combine to produce each situation count individually for no more than the individual cells of a tree.

By contrast, Schumpeter thought that economic growth could not be taken for granted like the growth of a tree, and that it depended on the attention paid to novelty in any economy.

Schumpeter's definition of novelty (innovation) is very broad. It includes five cases:

1. The introduction of a new good or service—that is, one with which consumers are not yet familiar—or a new quality of an existing good or service.
2. The introduction of a new method of production or a new way of handling a commodity commercially.
3. The opening of a new marketing area, that is, a market into which the good or service in question has not previously entered.

4. The conquest of a new source of supply of raw materials or half-manufactured goods.
5. A new method of organization in any industry.

The economic progress of humanity depends heavily upon new kinds of goods and services. By contrast, only a small amount of progress can be made by simply working harder at making old things in old ways. Such was Schumpeter's central idea. It takes on special importance in this century in view of the "population explosion" which compels mankind to find ever more goods and services, not only to supply more individuals but also to try to meet "the revolution of rising expectations" within each individual. Death-control through better nutrition and better medical care is spreading around the world much faster than birth-control, and there is no apparent early end to this divergence. And people who live now much as their ancestors lived hundreds or even thousands of years ago are suddenly no longer willing to go on in the old dispensation. It is easy to see why economists regard innovation as a major component of capitalism.

The Great Industrial Families

Schumpeter felt that the highly competitive organization of industry which the classical economists favored would not promote enough innovation. He mentioned agriculture as among the most competitive industries and noted that almost no improvement in agriculture had come from within agriculture itself. The great modern improvements, he said, have come from "big business"—tractors from General Motors and Ford, farm machinery from International Harvester, chemicals from Dupont, etc.

The same is true, Schumpeter said, of other competitive

industries such as clothing. Firms in competitive industries seem to be too small and too bound by tradition to be major innovators. Schumpeter used to say to his classes at Harvard, "Greater competition in the lamp industry might have produced cheaper oil lamps, but never the electric light."

Schumpeter traced the source of innovating energy in the economy to those big businesses which are controlled by great industrial families—the Duponts, Rockefellers, Morgans, Fords, etc., and their counterparts in other nations. "As soon as we go into details," he writes, "and inquire into the individual items in which progress has been most conspicuous, the trail leads not to the doors of those firms that work under conditions of comparatively free competition, but precisely to the doors of large concerns . . . and a shocking suspicion dawns upon us that big business may have had more to do with creating our standard of life than with keeping it down."[1]

The last statement in that quotation was written in the early 1940's when conservatives like Schumpeter were still stinging under such names as "economic royalists," "lords of creation," and "robber barons" that so-called social reformers had applied to big-business men.

Schumpeter took an entirely different view of these families of great wealth. He saw them as working, generation after generation, to bring more and more products into mass production for the masses. He said that very rich people have little to gain for themselves from the mass production they create. Their achievement does not consist in providing electric light for kings or silk stockings for queens. On the contrary, innovation by the rich is notable for the cheap cloth, cheap cotton and synthetic fabrics, shoes, automobiles, air travel, antibiotics, vaccines, and the whole range of modern goods and services, which it brings to people of ordinary income in return for steadily decreasing amounts of effort.

What, then, motivates the great industrial families to put their capacity for innovation at the service of "the massses"? Schumpeter's answer was that certain men desire very deeply to found or perpetuate a great family which will go down through the generations in a position of industrial and social leadership. These industrialists work all their lives to build a great industry upon some new group of products or new methods of production or new areas of economic development or new kinds of industrial organization. They are obviously not working for their own pleasure, for beyond a certain point they have little to gain in personal consumption from additional wealth. Nor are they working in hope of later ease for they usually continue to work hard even when they become fantastically wealthy, and often die with their dictaphones on. Schumpeter thought that the "great family" motive was their strongest drive.

Prosperity and Depression

Schumpeter did not expect an innovating economy to grow as smoothly as a tree. He expected the growth process to be very bumpy indeed, and to consist of a roller-coaster type of movement which would persist as long as innovations were made, that is, as long as there was economic progress. He called these ups and downs "economic cycles," each consisting of two general phases, prosperity and depression.

Periods of prosperity, in Schumpeter's view, occur because of the "bunching" of innovations. Bunching occurs because the great industrial families tend to innovate at the same time, each encouraging the others. When the corporations of one such family start to expand in some new way, the others hear of it, and start something of their own to complement, supplement or compete. This movement spreads until a general wave of innovation is taking place, giving extensive employment to workers, machine makers, and builders, and putting plenty of money into consumers' pockets to the delight of retailers and wholesalers.

But there comes a time when the innovators stop expanding their enterprises in order to concentrate on using them to produce the innovated goods and services for profit. This brings about a drop in new orders to all persons engaged in the business of expanding economic facilities and they suffer depression. Depression also comes to those still making certain old products in old ways who now face inevitable defeat at the hands of the new. Schumpeter called such a period a time of "creative destruction," when the economic ground is being cleared of the old, and forces are being gathered for the next wave of innovation which will bring the next period of prosperity.

Schumpeter thus accepted the ups and downs of economic life as an integral part of economic progress, and he did not expect them to be eliminated, or want them to be aborted by public policies. For him, a depression was a plateau, a resting place, a regrouping operation, on the upward march of economic growth, and recovery would come only when the innovators were ready to begin a new phase of the ascent.

However, Schumpeter did recommend adequate support of the unemployed during depressions. He thought that the only really intolerable effect of depressions was the loss of income to the unemployed, and he said that this could easily be taken care of, out of the growing wealth that innovation brings, by maintaining the incomes of the unemployed. Society would not be justified, he said, in forcing one group of people to pay the whole price of its progress, and besides, they might become revolutionary.

The Tricycle Ride

Schumpeter's study of the history of prosperity and depression, going back for several centuries and summarized in the two large volumes of his *Business Cycles,* led him to conclude that innovation causes three cycles of economic ups and downs, each a different length, and all going at the same time, just as ocean waves ride on long sea swells, which in turn are mounted on the flow and ebb of tides.

The longest of these waves, Schumpeter said, takes about 55 years to complete its whole cycle of prosperity phase and depression phase combined. He called it the Kondratieff cycle, after the Russian economist who first observed it in the statistics. The innovating phase of this cycle, that is its prosperity phase, is associated with what historians call an Industrial Revolution. Thus the rise of a long wave from about 1787 to about 1800 corresponds to what textbooks call *the* Industrial Revolution. But, Schumpeter notes, this was followed by a downward sweep in economic activity ending about 1842. From that point there began another industrial revolution, based on further innovations, extending from 1843 to about 1857, and that ebbed away until 1897, to be followed by a new upward wave that reached its peak about 1911 and ebbed away until 1940. (Its end was obscured by World War II.) Schumpeter hoped that there would never be an end to this succession of industrial revolutions, each one of which brought new goods and services within reach of "the masses."

Each of these cycles of industrial revolution has within it, Schumpeter said, a major subcycle, which he called a Juglar after the French economist who first published definite proof of it. This economic cycle is sometimes as short as seven years from peak to peak, and sometimes as long as eleven years. Essentially each Juglar cycle represents an episode in the completion of the group of innovations being made in the current industrial revolution, as chapters are parts of a book. This cycle of intermediate length is what businessmen and politicians are talking about, usually, when they use the term business cycle.

The shortest cycle, taking about forty months to complete all its phases, Schumpeter called a Kitchin cycle, after the English economist who gave the first clear demonstration of it.

All of these cycles of prosperity and depression operate in an environment of general history. Wars, famines, plagues, revolutions, and political changes may distort them in various ways but, in the Schumpeterian theory, these ups and downs are the natural walk of economic progress.

One historical dividend of this "three-cycle schema," as Schumpeter called it, is an answer to the question of why some depressions are so deep. The Great Depression of the 1930's, for example, was so "great" that capitalism was nearly overthrown as a system. Yet until then there had not been a really depressing depression since the mid-1890's. The minor "crises" of 1907 and 1921 had lasted less than a year, and a false sense of security had been created that the liability of capitalism to depressions was a misery of the past. This optimism was crushed under the weight of falling values from 1929 to 1933, and even by 1939 only a partial recovery had occurred. It was the outbreak of World War II which abolished that depression, to the benefit of capitalism in some ways, but also to its shame that a peaceful tool for recovery had not been found.

Schumpeter said that a low point such as that of the

winter of 1932-1933, which saw unemployment rise above 33 per cent in most of the capitalist nations, was the conjuncture of low points of all three of his cycles. The long cycle was near its greatest depth, the middle cycle at its lowest, and even the short cycle, in that grim winter, was at its most depressed. (It was the winter in which Hitler came to power in Germany.) There had been similar low points in the 1830's, 1870's, 1890's, and in preceding centuries, but somehow they had not shaken the world as the Great Depression did, unless one wishes to notice that Marx made his law of the increasing severity of depressions and his law of the increasing misery of the proletariat under capitalism partly out of his observations during the deep depressions of the nineteenth century.

Another dividend paid to our understanding by Schumpeter's three-cycle theory concerns the relationship of the prosperity phase of any cycle to the following depression. Our folklore assures us that the higher we go the harder we fall, what goes up must come down, the bigger the drunk, the worse the hangover, and so on. In the ups and downs of prosperity and depression, however, as we look back over several centuries, we find that periods of intense prosperity are followed by mild depressions and periods of mild prosperity by deep depressions.

Schumpeter's theory explains this by relating such cycles to the underlying cycle of longer period. For example, when a Juglar cycle (seven to eleven years) is occurring on the upswing phase of a Kondratieff cycle (about fifty-five years), the underlying upward movement of the longer cycle both intensifies the prosperity phase of the Juglar and moderates its depression phase. And when the longer cycle is moving downward, this puts a drag on the prosperity phase of the shorter cycle and also deepens its depression phases.

The Fate of Capitalism

In spite of the roller-coaster ride of capitalism, Schumpeter felt that it was far and away the best economic system ever devised for improving the lot of ordinary people. Over the past century and a half, he noted, the standard of living per person in the advanced capitalist nations had gone up 2 or 3 per cent per year. Nothing so generous had ever occurred before in the history of man, and if capitalism were allowed to go on like that for another generation or two, Schumpeter said, the average standard of living would exceed everything social reformers were demanding. Even maintaining the incomes of the unemployed during depressions would by then be "a light burden."

What could prevent capitalism from going on? Schumpeter had a one-word answer for that—democracy. He felt that the "masses" were becoming too impatient with capitalism. As the "revolution of rising expectations" gathered force, this impatience would persuade people of ordinary income to turn to Socialism or Communism, which would ultimately leave them poorer, or turn them to New Dealism, which would be so hostile to the great industrial families that innovation would stop. It was horrifying to Schumpeter to see so many intellectuals helping to lead the masses into this impatience trap. Labor unions, he thought, made matters worse by "interfering with the discipline of the working classes." If the workers only knew the truth, Schumpeter said, they would realize that "the long-run interests of society are entirely lodged with the upper strata of bourgeois society."

As a substitute for democracy, Schumpeter did not advocate any kind of Fascism or Nazism. He had no confidence in the ability to govern of upstart dictators. And the abilities of businessmen, even the richest, to rule nations, he rated lowest of all. He wrote in *Capitalism, Socialism and Democracy:*

> There is surely no trace of mystic glamour about the businessman, which is what counts in the ruling of men. The stock exchange is a poor substitute for the Holy Grail. . . . Nor are his experiences and habits of life of the kind that develop personal fascination. A genius in the business office may be, and often is, utterly unable, outside of it, to say boo to a goose in the drawing room and on the platform. Knowing this he wants to be left alone and to leave politics alone.[2]

The graduate students in Schumpeter's classes used to ask him from time to time what form of government he considered ideal. His answer always referred to the Austro-Hungarian Empire when its center was the Vienna of the glamorous waltzes. He remembered his own experience with the courtly grace of those times, the homage paid to great professors even at Court, the cultured mingling of many nationalities under a benign and permissive Emperor, and in Vienna the brightly-shining shop windows showing new products, only a block or two away from the carefully kept gardens and fountains of an older time.

Even the electric streetcars were not unharmonious in old Vienna, passing the big cafés where people sat discussing politics over coffee topped with whipped cream. There were flower boxes in the windows around the square. And in the suburbs and the narrow valleys where the cold streams flowed, industrial geniuses were producing the innovations that would in a generation or two eliminate poverty, if only one let them alone. How could such a "perfect" society fall?

One reason, suggested to Schumpeter by some of his students, was that his ideal governments, consisting of aristocrats with "mystic glamour" acting as "fronts" for innovating industrial families, historically showed tendencies to make periodic armed tours of other people's countries, thus provoking resentments and wars. The kaisers of Germany, the emperors of Japan, some of the kings of England and of Spain, and the Hapsburg emperors themselves confirmed this habit. Schumpeter always responded to this objection with obvious impatience, even advising the objector to go home and get some sleep and hope to see things more clearly upon awakening. Schumpeter thought of war and imperialism as medieval survivals which he expected to see disappear if capitalism continued. Some of the nations of the world with the highest standards of living, he noted, have not in recent history been either warlike or imperialistic, including Sweden, Denmark, Canada, Australia, New Zealand, and Switzerland.

Permanent Innovation

Economists are grateful to Professor Schumpeter for adding innovation as a component of our picture of capitalism and showing its relation to industrial revolutions, economic cycles, the great industrial families, and the welfare of the "masses." But our ideas about the innovation procedure have been growing since he wrote.

For one thing, we recognize that the innovating groups in our economy include others besides the great industrial families idolized by Schumpeter. To see the whole picture of the groups involved in innovation as it now is, examine Diagram I.

The diagram starts with religious leaders and philosophers since they must create a climate of thought favorable to innovation. Then come scientific theorists who propose the existence of various patterns of order and control in Nature, as Einstein proposed the relationship $E=MC^2$, or

Pasteur the germ-theory of disease, or Faraday the phenomenon of electricity. These propositions are tested by scientific researchers who accumulate masses of research about Nature which stimulate modifications of old theories and the creation of new ones and their testing in turn by additional research.

DIAGRAM I

THE INNOVATION PROCEDURE

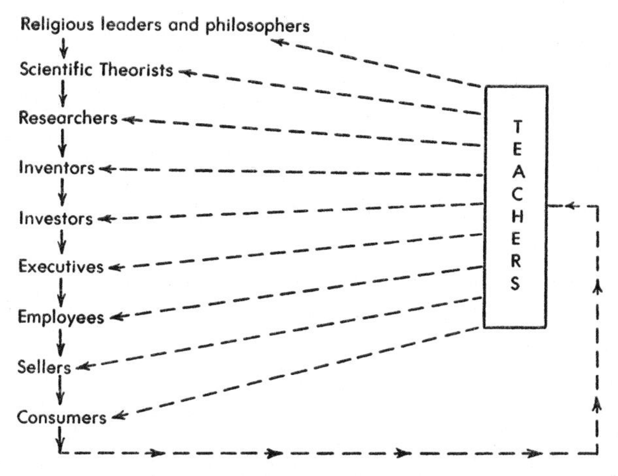

Note: Solid arrows show the main flow of ideas, facts, goods, and services through the innovational process. Dotted arrows show the flow of persons. Subsidiary flows, not shown, occur between all groups, but are instrumental to the main flows shown above.

It is on the basis of the facts turned up by research that inventors do their work. Edison made the electric light after years of studying the existing body of scientific facts about glass, metals, vacuums, heat, light, and electricity. Atomic machines first appeared some forty years after Einstein's theory had been announced and were based upon accumulated research into atomic behavior. Modern chemical inventions for the control of disease have arisen from the immense researches which followed Pasteur's ideas.

Next comes the more strictly business phase of the procedure of innovation. Investors look over the crop of new and old inventions and decide how much money, if any, to devote to their manufacture. They turn the actual administrative work over to executives who organize employees to do the actual work. Then sellers take over.

Consumers seem to be a relatively passive group in the innovation process. They did not demand TV or steamships or vaccines by mass demonstrations or other signs of discontent before their appearance. The consumer waits to be impressed by sellers before changing to new goods or services.

In another respect consumers are not passive, since, if innovation is to continue, they must present themselves to teachers who will train them to take their places in one or another of the innovational groups as Diagram I indicates. In this way the process becomes a permanent part of the economy.

Another new direction in our interest in innovation as one component of capitalism is a broadening of the concept itself. We have been grateful to Schumpeter for making it as broad as he did—including not only new goods and services and new methods of production, but also new kinds of organization, new markets, and new sources of supply. However, as we have coped with the total effect of the modern "gale of innovation," as he called it, we have come to see the need for new social innovations to match the economic ones. For example, the automobile is useful and fun, but to keep it from choking the streets and our lungs we shall have to have new designs for the centers of our cities. The production of atomic energy requires the innovation of new methods of achieving security, both national and international. Universal education, to take another example, requires new plans for safeguarding the quality of education for the bright children. And so on. Many economic innovations require social innovation to secure their best uses.

Challenge to the Rich

Schumpeter's connection between the great industrial families and innovation points to a possible solution of a significant modern problem—the question of the economic function of the rich. Wealthy families seem to develop in every free society and in past centuries, these families have found acceptable economic functions as protectors, patrons, and statesmen.

In this century in many countries the traditional duties of the rich have been taken over by other groups and their power and numbers whittled away. In Russia and China, millions of property owners, even down to very modest levels, have been killed by the government. And in the theory of democratic Socialism, which has a very wide appeal around the world, it is proposed to nationalize some of the holdings of wealthy families and to confiscate the rest by supertaxes on income and inheritance. In England where these policies have already been started, some propertied families have been reduced to acting as tourist guides through their own castles.

However, in some of the democracies, there are rich families who have found a new function to replace the old —by taking a major share in innovating. This has been true, for example, in Sweden, the United States, and West Germany. The Dupont family in the United States is the best-known model of this Schumpeterian adaptation, but there are thousands of such cases if one includes the prominent local families of the many cities scattered across the land.

Where this adaptation has taken place, there seems to be general public acceptance of the wealth of the wealthy, because it is being used for the public good. Even among the rich the idea is abroad that their wealth is something they hold in trust *pro bono publico*. There is often found among them an attitude of *richesse oblige*, not in the sense of conveying their wealth to charity, but rather of devoting themselves to innovation.

If such a commitment could be made generally by the rich of all nations, the Marxian Law of Class Struggle might be breached. Marx taught that the rich have always lived as parasites upon the poor and must be overthrown violently unless they abdicate of their own free will. Marx even declared this class struggle to be the central process of human history.

Unfortunately, there are many areas of the world where the rich have not committed themselves to this new function. One thinks of Central and South America, of parts of Africa, of the Middle East, of India, and of the nations of southeast Asia, as places where most of the rich still hold forth in old ways, assuming a royal or divine prerogative to be of no particular use.

It is in these nations that the cries of the Marxists against the rich are listened to most seriously. For their own sakes and for the sake of the good they can do with their resources of time, money, education, and influence, we may hope for an awakening among the families of this overworld.

Fortunately the technique of being an investor in the innovational process is well enough known that the rich who accept the challenge can educate themselves and their children to perform the role. The requirements of such work are that the investor keep in touch with three or four of the other innovating groups. He must know what models of new things inventors have produced in whatever area of innovation he may choose to specialize. He must know executives whom he can hire to organize production. And he must be in contact with consumers directly or indirectly to maximize the acceptability of the new things. These three sets of contacts will be enough unless his motivation fails now and again. In that case, he will need to be in touch with religious leaders and philosophers, who can help him with "the struggle for meaning" in life.

CHAPTER 4

Abolishing Depressions: the element of full employment

The third essential element in our formula for successful capitalism was added by John Maynard Keynes (1883-1946). Keynes said that capitalism needs a central procedure for preventing depressions and assuring full employment.

The importance of such a procedure is that without it, capitalism, as a combination of freedom and prosperity, will very probably be overthrown during some deep, intractable worldwide depression of the kind that overtook the capitalist world in the decade of the 1930's, and that had overtaken it several times in the nineteenth century.

It appears now that the Keynesian procedure will not need to be used as continuously as Keynes expected, and that it need not involve the degree of control over the institutions of private investment that Keynes thought would be necessary. Consequently there is less need for alarm about Keynesianism than conservatives once felt.

The Repeal of Say's Law

What Keynes did was to cause the repeal of Say's Law, and this was a bitter draught for those who had hoped that the government need never again play a major part in economic life. Say had demonstrated to the satisfaction of the classical economists that if unemployment on any substantial scale developed in the capitalist system, it would disappear of its own accord if the workers involved were classical economic men. The workers would simply compete with one another and drive wages down to the point where it would be profitable for businessmen to employ them even under depressed economic conditions. Their re-employment would then raise their incomes as consumers and lift the depression. It was an automatic mechanism, like clockwork.

In the famous Chapter 19 of his *General Theory of Employment, Interest and Money* (1936), Keynes took the clock apart to see why it was not working in the Great Depression. His conclusion was that it did not work because it had no works; capitalism had no built-in tendency to restore its own equilibrium at or near full employment when depression afflicted it.

Wage reductions, which were supposed to be the mainspring of the classical mechanism, were more likely, Keynes said, to increase unemployment in depressed times. Their first effect would be to reduce workers' incomes, and this would be translated into lower consumer spending, a naturally depressive influence upon business. Furthermore, one reduction in wage costs usually creates expectations of further reductions later on. Businessmen would therefore postpone some planned investments in order to take advantage of lower costs in the future. Consumers, too, seeing wages fall, and expecting reductions in prices, would postpone purchases of durable goods such as homes, cars, and appliances. All of this would affect business adversely.

Also, Keynes noted, the movement toward lower wages and prices would increase the burden of debt on business and consumers. Debts are usually stated in fixed money terms, and if a downward wage-price spiral occurs, it becomes harder to meet payments of principal and interest.

Altogether, Keynes concluded, depressions were likely to be made even deeper by the operation of the classical mechanism.

Keynes did concede that perhaps an overall reduction of wages, made once and for all, with no possibility of repetition, affecting all workers, and accompanied by a similar scaling down of prices and debts, might at some carefully selected time moderate a depression. But that kind of action would be an aspect of a planned economy which Keynes did not recommend.

Was Keynes a Socialist?

What then is capitalism to do with this possibly fatal tendency to depressions?

Keynes's full answer was threefold: (1) use government spending in excess of taxes (deficit spending) to get a depressed economy going again, (2) reduce the inequalities in the distribution of wealth by taxation of the rich in order to put more money into the hands of those who would spend it more quickly, and (3) act on financial institutions with a view to reducing interest rates, and on the stock market to reduce the instabilities caused by overemphasis on speculation.

Conservatives have often called Keynes a Socialist. To an economist, a Socialist is a man who believes in government ownership of all enterprises, if one takes the traditional definition, or government ownership of the "commanding heights" of the economy—steel, railroads, road transport, banks, public utilities, etc.—if one takes the modified view adopted by many British Socialists. Keynes denied that he favored Socialism in either of these senses. Those of us who, as graduate students at Cambridge, regularly attended his lectures and also spoke with him personally, heard him deny it many times.

For the reader, Keynes put his thoughts on this issue into the final chapter of the *General Theory of Employment, Interest and Money,* a chapter with the title "Concluding Notes on the Social Philosophy Towards which the General Theory Might Lead." Perhaps the reader would like to hear Keynes defending himself against the charge of Socialism in his own words taken from that chapter:

> When 9,000,000 men are employed out of 10,000,000 willing and able to work, there is no evidence that the labour of these 9,000,000 men is misdirected. The complaint against the present system is not that these 9,000,000 men should be employed on different tasks but that tasks should be available for the remaining 1,000,000 men.
>
> No obvious case is made out for a system of State Socialism which would embrace most of the economic life of the community. It is not the ownership of the instruments of production which it is important for the State to assume. If the State is able to determine the aggregate amount of resources devoted to augmenting the instruments and the basic rate of reward to those who own them, it will have accomplished all that is necessary.
>
> I conceive therefore that a somewhat comprehensive socialization of investment will prove the only means of securing an approximation to full employment.[1]

The issue of Keynes's beliefs is partly clouded by his prescription of "a somewhat comprehensive socialization of investment." There he actually has used the word socialization, with respect to one part of the economy, but he diluted it with the preceding rather strange adjective-phrase "somewhat comprehensive."

Keynes's career hardly fitted our accustomed image of a Socialist. For one thing, he made five million dollars largely by speculating in the stock market. And, he was head of one of the largest private insurance companies in Great Britain, the National Mutual Life Assurance Society. He was also a director of a notably conservative institution, that "Old Lady of Threadneedle Street," the Bank of England. All this was in addition to his teaching duties at Cambridge University, where he was also the bursar who made King's College rich by guiding its investments in securities. Even when he tried not to make a profit, as in the publication of a series of economic classics, the money rolled in. Politically, Keynes often met with leaders of the Liberal Party, and was even more often a consultant to the British government, whether Conservative or Labor. For his advice and accomplishments, he was made Lord Keynes of Tilton.

Keynes seemed to have set as his personal ideal the cultural life of a nobleman of the Renaissance. He married Lydia Lopokova, famed as a great beauty and as a dancer with the Imperial Ballet of St. Petersburg and with Diaghilev's company. Together they established the Vic-Wells Ballet. Keynes also used part of his personal fortune to build and donate to Cambridge University a theater for all the performing arts. He was a trustee of the National Gallery, and he founded, with Samuel Courtauld, the London Artists Association. In literary affairs, Keynes was a leading personality of the famous Bloomsbury Group, a salon of illustrious writers and artists that included Lytton Strachey, Virginia Woolf, and Leonard Woolf.

If all this was the life of a Socialist, Keynes made the most of it in a highly capitalistic way.

The Money Goes Around and Around

Keynes wanted us to see our economy as a single system. The classical economists had sought to start with the bits and pieces of the economy—the individual worker, the individual businessman, the individual consumer—and with these parts, they tried to build up a picture of the whole economy. Keynes wanted to start at the opposite end, beginning with the whole economy and working down to the ultimate effects on individuals. (The classical method is now called "microeconomics." Keynes's method is called "macroeconomics.")

In Keynes's overall picture of our economy there are three basic groups of people—consumers, businessmen, and workers. (In the term "workers" we include all who receive an income from business—whether it be wages, salaries, rent, interest, or dividends.) As illustrated in the lower half of Diagram II, these groups are all dependent upon a basic circulation of money moving between them which causes a flow of goods and services to move in the opposite direction. Consumers take their money to the businessmen, who provide them goods and services in return. Businessmen pay money to the workers (as defined above), who give their services to the employers' businesses in return. And the workers take their paychecks home to their consuming families and friends, who supply the worker with the rewards of family life and friendship. The consumers also find time to renew the whole circular flow by taking the money to the businessmen again.

DIAGRAM II

Money Pressure

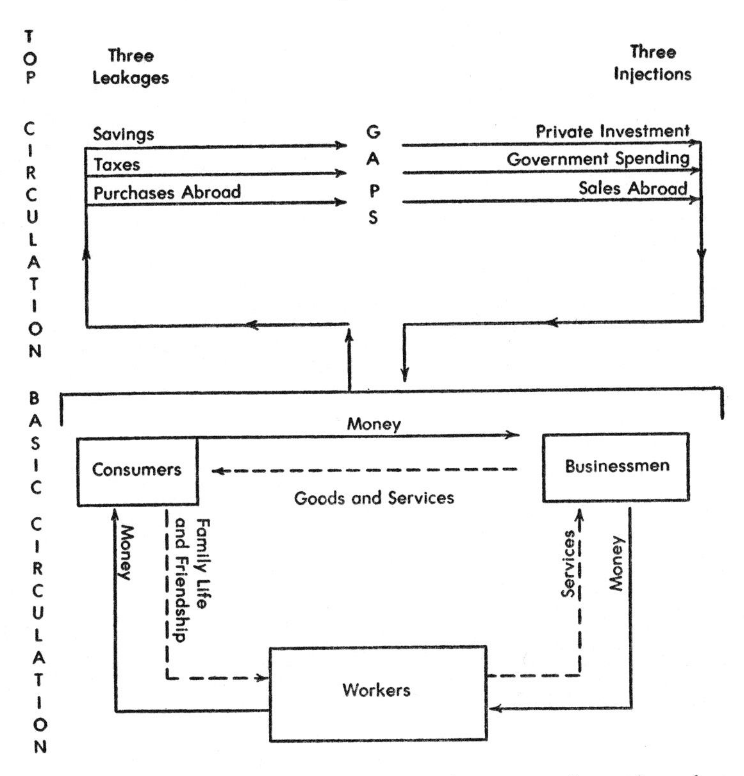

This system looks like a form of perpetual motion, but in fact it is vulnerable to depression because of leakages. As illustrated in the top half of Diagram II, these leakages take the form of

1. Savings
2. Taxes
3. Purchases abroad

All three of the basic groups leak some of their money in each of these ways.

Protection against the depression which these leakages may cause exists in three compensators which inject money into the circulation:

1. Private investment
2. Government spending
3. Sales abroad

When the sum of these three injections of money exceeds the sum of the three leakages, then the monetary flow in the economy is increasing and employment will go up. On the other hand, when the sum of the leakages exceeds the sum of the injections, then monetary pressure in the economy will fall and so will employment. (This double proposition might well be called Keynes's Law or the Keynesian Amendment to classical economic theory, replacing Say's Law.)

Protection against depression consists of a procedure for lowering the leakages and increasing the injections whenever the leakages exceed, or threaten to exceed, the injections.

The classical economists thought that there were automatic responses in the economy which would make savings equal to investment and purchases abroad equal to sales abroad, though perhaps there would be an interval during which gaps would persist. And the classical economists hoped that moral and political prudence would make government spending not greater than taxation.

Keynesian analysis says, on the contrary, that the gaps between the leakages and the injections may persist indefinitely, doing great harm to the economy unless there is a procedure for changing them.

Keynes put special emphasis upon the point that the

savings leakage may be either greater or less than the investment injection. This is because decisions to save are made for different reasons and usually by different people than decisions to invest.

Decisions to save are made by individuals, businesses, and governments. Individuals save for personal reasons which Keynes lists under eight headings, calling them the motives of "precaution, foresight, calculation (enjoyment of interest), improvement, independence, enterprise, pride, and avarice." Businesses and governments put money aside for four reasons, Keynes says, to secure resources for expansion, to have funds to tide over difficult times, to have a source of income other than the business, and to take care of obsolescence.

Decisions to invest, on the other hand, are made for quite another set of reasons, according to Keynes. The main influence upon any decision to make an additional investment is the estimated prospective gain from the investment as compared with its cost. (Keynes has coined a rather bothersome term for this prospective gain—he calls it "the marginal efficiency of capital." Such coinage of clumsy terms is an annoying habit of many important economists.) The investor then compares this expected gain with the rate of interest on the amount of money involved. If the rate of interest is higher than the expected gain, it will pay the investor to forego the investment and lend his money to someone else. If the rate of interest is lower than the expected gain, it will pay the investor to put his own money, plus whatever he needs to borrow, into the investment under consideration.

It is clear, said Keynes, when we take account of the different motives for saving and the different motives for investing, that significant gaps may develop between the savings leakage and the injection of investment.

It is clear also that the tax-leakage may be either overcompensated or undercompensated by government spending. The government can spend more than its tax-take by borrowing the difference. In return for this borrowed money the government gives IOU's, called bonds, or notes, and the total of these bonds and notes outstanding at any time is government debt. If government spending is less than its tax-take, then the treasury accumulates a surplus.

We know, too, that the foreign leakage can be overcompensated or undercompensated by the amount of goods and services foreigners buy from us. (Note that economists, when speaking of the foreign leakage, include all our payments made to foreigners, including trade and credit, tourist spending, shipping charges, insurance payments, dividends and interest—in brief, all payments to foreigners, and on the compensating side all payments coming in the other direction.) If there is an excess of payments going out, then a nation loses gold if it is on the gold standard for international payments, or if it is not, the value of its money declines in relation to foreign monies. But if there is an excess of payments coming in, then the nation receives gold or sees the relative value of its money rise.

Such is the overall picture of capitalism, as Keynes saw it, a circulation of money and products among three basic groups of people—consumers, workers, and businessmen—with the circulation subject to depression by three major leakages, and restored to health (if the right policies are followed) by three compensating injections.

Keynes's Pessimism About Private Investment

Economists of nearly all varieties of political belief have accepted Keynes's overall picture of capitalism as a major contribution to our understanding of our system. But when it comes to Keynes's policy recommendations, deep differences of opinion have shown themselves.

The root of these differences is Keynes's pessimism about private investment as a compensator for the savings leakage. Keynes felt that the more highly developed and wealthy an economy becomes, the fewer opportunities for profitable investment will remain. This idea became known as "the mature economy thesis" or "the stagnation thesis."

How Keynes came by this idea no one seems to know. It may have stemmed from his experience of the Great Depression of the 1930's when good private investments were hard to find. Or it may have come from the special experience of England where the Great Depression started several years earlier, and seemed more intractable than elsewhere. Keynes himself stated his reasons as follows:

> During the nineteenth century, the growth of population and of invention, the opening up of new lands, the state of confidence and the frequency of war over the average of [say] each decade seem to have been sufficient, taken in conjunction with the propensity to consume, to establish a schedule of the marginal efficiency of capital which allowed a reasonably satisfactory level of employment to be compatible with a rate of interest high enough to be psychologically acceptable to wealth owners. . . . Today and presumably for the future, the schedule of the marginal efficiency of capital is, for a variety of reasons, much lower than it was in the nineteenth century.[2]

One might observe, from the vantage point of the 1960's, that there seems to be no shortage in the twentieth century of the factors Keynes mentions as encouraging economic growth in the nineteenth—"growth of population and of invention, the opening up of new lands, the state of confidence and the frequency of war." However, Keynes was so sure that capitalism had reached the end of its era of expansion that he riveted his policy recommendations to that assumption.

Perhaps the single most significant statement in *The General Theory of Employment, Interest and Money* is on page 245, where Keynes states his stagnationist assumptions. This statement occurs at the beginning of a chapter called "The General Theory of Employment Restated," and reads as follows:

> We have now reached a point where we can gather together the threads of our argument. To begin with, it may be useful to make clear which elements in the economic system we usually take as given, which are the independent variables of our system and which are the dependent variables. We take as given the existing quality and quantity of available labor, the existing quality and quantity of available equipment, the existing technique, the degree of competition, the tastes and habits of the consumer, the disutilities of different intensities of labour and of the activities of supervision and organization, as well as the social structure, including the forces, other than our variables set forth below, which determine the distribution of the national income. This does not mean that we assume these factors to be constant; but merely that in this place and context we are not considering on taking into account the effects and consequences of changes in them.[3]

The last sentence of that quotation seems to indicate that Keynes may have intended at some later time to free the quantities he took as given in the *General Theory of Employment, Interest and Money*. In the remaining ten years of his life he did not do so, but those were years of world crisis, hard work, and deep fatigue for him. It is interesting to note that Keynes's parents survived him and both lived to be nearly a hundred. By the ordinary probabilities, Keynes, who died at 63, should have had much more time.

As matters stand, the assumptions remain frozen in Keynes's theory, and it hardly needs an economist to see that if all these things that Keynes mentions are held constant, there will be very little opportunity for profitable investment. Keynes's working model of the economy was therefore a stagnant model. Stagnation was its assumption rather than a conclusion of its logic.

Keynes's assumptions may be summarized by saying that they exclude the whole "innovational frontier" of economic life as Schumpeter defined it. Schumpeter himself remarked upon this in his *History of Economic Analysis*. In a critique of Keynes's theory, he asks the reader to "observe that the restrictive assumptions in question exclude the very essence of capitalist reality, all the phenomena and problems of which—including the short-run phenomena and problems—hinge upon the incessant creation of new and novel capital equipment."[4]

Why Conservatives Dislike Keynes

There may be some conservatives who admire Keynes, but if so, their voices have not been publicly audible. Some conservatives dislike him because they believe he was a Socialist, bent upon undermining and destroying our economic freedoms. We have presented reasons for the conclusion that Keynes did not view himself in that light and that such conservatives show misunderstanding of Keynes's intentions. Anti-Keynesians reply that his effects will be socialistic, whatever his intentions. But if that is the way things turn out, it could only be because, as Schumpeter used to say to his classes, "Gentlemen, history sometimes plays jokes upon us which are not always in good taste."

Still, there were and are substantial reasons for conservatives to dislike Keynes. All of them arise from the fact that Keynes was trying to keep a capitalistic economy in operation under the assumption that it no longer had a frontier, either geographical or technological, along which it could advance economically. This assumption led Keynes to the view that the net savings leakage would tend to grow steadily greater. Consequently he proposed rather drastic public policies to reduce savings, increase investment, and lower the rate of interest.

Keynes's attack upon present levels of saving in the developed nations has been received with great hostility by conservatives. The word "saving" is almost sacred in the American tradition as the means by which budding enterprise gets its start, the means by which individuals tide over emergencies in their middle years, and the means to be independent and comfortable in old age. Yet Keynes showed that, whatever advantages saving might give one individual over another, there was a point beyond which it would no longer benefit the economy, and that was the point at which the saving was not able to find its way back into the economic mainstream through investment.

Keynes noted that whenever additional saving occurs it is bound to be depressive to the economy, since businessmen experience a loss of business at once. This could only be beneficial if the economy were suffering from high money-pressure (excessive inflation) as, for example, during wartime. In normal times, as Keynes expected normal to be, that is, with a substantial amount of unemployment, the loss of business might so lower the businessman's expectation of gain from his investment that he would be less willing to invest than before. Thus the saving, even though it would provide funds to make more investment possible, would actually make more investment less likely than if the money had been spent.

The reader who sees capitalism in the Keynesian manner as nourished by circulations of goods, services, and money may play a little game to see what savings can do. To make the effect larger, suppose that in some year the public decides to save half its income. The sudden switch of money-flow from business to banks would fill the banks with savings, but business would be so depressed that businessmen would lay off, say, half of the working force. Half of the consumers would then have to draw out their savings to live on, until the savings were exhausted. In the end, there might well be less savings than the original amounts, even though the public had started out to save a great deal more. This should teach us that, like the circulation of blood in our bodies, the economic circulation is interconnected by its various flows of money and we must trace any change in one flow through the whole system before we can judge its effects.

Keynes's proposals to reduce savings in a "mature" economy included a sharp reduction in the wealth of the wealthy, to be achieved by high taxes on income and wealth. These taxes would be spent on the lower-income group, who regularly spend a higher proportion of their money than the rich. It is not too astonishing that the rich have never been enthusiastic about Keynes.

Towards the same end, Keynes proposed to reduce the rate of interest as close to zero as possible by having the government collect the savings of people and institutions and make them available as loans for business investment at a rate as close to zero as possible. This would eliminate the class of people who are professional savers, that is, who save money in order to live off the interest. In Europe such people are call "rentiers" (in America, "coupon-clippers"), and Keynes described his policy as "the euthanasia of the rentier." It would eliminate another source of saving—and another segment of conservative power.

Keynes also proposed to reform the stock market by making it more difficult for an individual to keep switching his holdings from one stock to another to take advantage of speculative trends. The stock market is one major artery through which savings become investments, and Keynes was disturbed that it should be used by so many stockholders as a gambling machine. He wrote: "When the capital development of a country becomes a by-product of the activities of a casino, the job is likely to be ill-done."[5]

Since Keynes made a great sum of money in the stock market, his description of it is especially interesting. His criticism is that professional investors who should be seeking to channel their money into the securities of firms which have the best growth possibilities in the long run are instead occupied in hopping from stock to stock trying to guess which ones will be in fashion with the next wave of speculation. Professional investment, he says, is like an English newspaper beauty competition in which the readers have to try to choose from among photographs the prettiest girl—not the one each thinks is really the prettiest, but the one each thinks the others will pick as the prettiest. The winners are the contestants who best guess what average opinion will be. In the stock market, Keynes says, "we have reached the third degree where we devote our intelligence to anticipating what average opinion expects average opinion to be. And there are some, I believe, who practise the fourth, fifth and higher degrees."[6] (In that same paragraph Keynes remarks, probably with a side-glance at his own speculative successes, "There is a peculiar zest in making money quickly.")

Keynes's proposal to make it harder for people to change their portfolios of stocks was not popular with investors and stockholders, and this cost him the respect of another body of usually conservative political opinions.

Actually, Keynes earned the dislike of all businessmen by his disparaging analysis of their "money-making passion." What he was trying to show was that businessmen had an inner drive which would keep them at work even if much of their profit was taken away. He declared himself in favor of leaving them some of it, since,

> Dangerous human proclivities can be canalized into comparatively harmless channels by the existence of opportunities for moneymaking and private wealth, which, if they cannot be satisfied in this way, may find their outlet in cruelty, the reckless pursuit of personal power and authority, and other forms of self-aggrandizement.[7]

It is obvious that this is not the light in which businessmen see themselves, and they have resented Keynes's view. To account for it, we must return again to those fateful assumptions on page 245 of the *General Theory*. If an economic system is operating as the Keynesian system is there described, without changes in the quality or quantity of available equipment, technique, competition, labor, supervision, organization, and consumers' tastes and habits, then there is very little for businessmen to do. For in real life they do in fact spend most of their time, thought, and energy in trying to change these very things.

What to Do

Even without Keynes's stagnationist assumptions a free economy is subject to recurring depressions. As Schumpeter showed, the innovation procedure produces waves of prosperity and depression of varying intensities and depths, and our economy needs an anti-depression procedure to ward them off. Schumpeter thought it would be better simply to let the economy ride through depressions, but the experience of the 1930's indicates that this is much too dangerous a policy.

What capitalism needs, therefore, is a method of reducing the leakages and increasing the injections when depression exists or threatens.

When that happens, the savings-investment gap can be influenced by trying to maintain consumer confidence and by encouraging business to invest. Low interest rates and an easier attitude by banks towards loans to businessmen are the primary tools here. The government can make more money available for loans by buying securities for its own portfolio, and by reducing the reserve requirements of the banks and loosening credit restrictions.

At the same time, the gap between purchases abroad and sales abroad can be influenced by all the measures we are familiar with for discouraging spending abroad and encouraging foreigners to buy more from us. There are somewhat narrow limits to this influence because it almost always brings retaliation from foreign countries which are trying to change the balance in the opposite direction.

One nation can gain a significant advantage by making its money cheaper for foreigners to buy (devaluation), but, again, there is the risk that other countries may do the same, thus cancelling the initial advantage. If an agreement can be reached among the major nations that such a cheapening is needed to enable a nation to keep its proper place in the world economy, and they promise not to retaliate, then devaluation can be an effective anti-depression tool. Unfortunately, devaluation may be hard on the emotions of those who have formed a patriotic or moral attachment to the existing price of the mark, the pound, the dollar, or whatever in relation to other national currencies. They may confuse "defending the dollar" with defending some specific price set for the dollar when conditions were different.

The most controllable and most powerful anti-depression tool is to influence the taxation-government spending gap, by reducing taxation or increasing government spending or both.

Some conservatives are opposed to higher government spending to ward off depressions on the ground that when it was tried in the United States during the 1930's it failed to lift the nation out of the Great Depression.

The answer to this criticism is that the nation's experiments with this tool during the depression were too little, too late, and too limited.

By the time President Roosevelt took office in March, 1933, the depression had been worsening since 1929 and had reduced the incomes of all residents of the United States from about 100 billion dollars a year in 1929 to about 60 billion dollars a year in 1932. The annual loss was therefore about 40 billion dollars. Against this Mr. Roosevelt ran small federal deficits as follows:

(fiscal year)	1933—3.0	billion	dollars
"	1934—4.6	"	"
"	1935—1.6	"	"
"	1936—5.1	"	"
"	1937—2.6	"	"
"	1938—0.8	"	"
"	1939—3.2	"	"
"	1940—2.6	"	"

Such a tiny and erratic governmental attack upon a depression of that magnitude could not hope to succeed.

Fortunately, as Keynes indicated, the governmental attack does not have to be equal to the annual loss of income caused by a depression. A dollar injected into the economy will add to one person's income and then to another's and another's as it passes from hand to hand or from bank account to bank account during the year. Part of the dollar will go into the leakages and not get back into the main spending flow, but by the end of the year the injected dollar may have increased incomes by, say, three dollars.

If the annual income multiplier had actually been 3 on the average for dollars injected by the United States government during the Great Depression, then the federal budget deficit required to make up a 40 billion dollar loss in incomes would have been a little over 13 billion dollars, at least in the first year with, hopefully, diminishing amounts in subsequent years as the economy responded.

Another factor lessening the amount of injection necessary is that new spending, as it goes through the arteries of the economy, may induce some new private investment. This is less likely to happen if businessmen are under fire from the government as "robber barons, lords of creation, and economic royalists," as they were during the 1930's. It is doubtless true that some business activities needed reform at that time, and that business generally needed to accept some channelling of its activities, but, as Keynes himself emphasized, "the state of confidence" is an important ingredient in decisions to make long-term investments, and political attitudes influence confidence.

World War II showed the United States how rapidly an economy can rise from depression to high activity (even overactivity) if the injection of government expenditure is large enough. Remembering the ineffective federal deficits of the 1930's, observe the deficits the government incurred during the years of World War II:

(fiscal year)	1941— 6	billion	dollars
"	1942—23.4	"	"
"	1943—64.3	"	"
"	1944—64.3	"	"
"	1945—57.7	"	"
"	1946—10.7	"	"

These figures, let the reader remember, are not total federal expenditures, but the excess of expenditures over tax receipts for each year.

Under the influence of these huge injections of government spending, the American economy shot up like a rocket. Large "surpluses" of grain, meat, milk, and fruits went down people's throats instead of being burned or poured into sand or left to rot as they had been only a few years before. Millions of the unemployed found work in the factories. Surplus farmers from Oklahoma and Arkansas were welcomed to California instead of being waved away as undesirables.

Of course, the amount of federal injections during the war was far larger than would have been necessary to bring recovery from the depression, and the result was a massive pile-up of new savings. This sum proved useful when the war ended, in that consumers and businessmen then had the money to keep the economy going briskly even after the federal injections stopped. In consequence, there was not the usual postwar depression. On the contrary, the United States suffered from high money-pressure for quite a few years after World War II.

We do not know how often a nation should use the anti-depression procedure, and this will undoubtedly be a much-discussed issue for decades. After the horrible experience of the Great Depression when the prosperity of the nations of the free world spiralled down, down, down for three full years to a level of incomes only about half what had been so recently achieved and to a level of unemployment of a third or more of the industrial population, there is a tendency now to use the procedure early and often. There is an obvious advantage to this, in that the expenditure is less if the depression is treated while it is still small or only threatening. Since so many slight ups and downs of the economy seem to correct themselves, however, the free nations may decide to experiment with fewer governmental injections.

But such problems are minor compared with the achievement of creating a procedure within each free nation to insure that depression will not again sweep over the free world as it did in the 1930's, bringing its storms of despair, dictatorship, destruction, and death.

CHAPTER 5

Sharing Control of the Economy: the element of countervailing power

The fourth component of successful capitalism is a system of countervailing power. This means that the decisions by which the economy is run, including political decisions, are made by organized groups which have a balanced-power relationship to one another. In the economy of the United States today, for example, we have powerful organizations in labor, agriculture, industry, government, education, law, medicine, science, and religion, all seeking, in their own various interests and according to their diverse lights, to influence the course of the economy. Organization is still weak among some groups—especially the consumers, the unemployed, the aged, and even among executives—but this may be corrected eventually.

All such groups are basically in harmony because of

their common interest in preserving and developing a free economy, but they are also partly in opposition to one another in competing for shares in the product and the power produced by the economy.

Another Human Experiment

We have called this system of groups another human experiment because it is a departure from the traditional way of managing human affairs. In the past, human communities have been in the habit of permitting one group in the economy to control the others. History from the most ancient times is a long record of ruling classes—militarists, landowners, priests, industrialists, merchants, guilds, imperialists, civil servants, and the rest. The attempts of one or another group to stay in the saddle, while riding roughshod over the other interests by the use of their moral, political, economic, and military powers, have taxed the memory of many a schoolboy. The purpose of introducing countervailing power into capitalism is to remove these age-old dominations and exploitations.

The classical economists hoped to take care of the problem of economic power in another way. In the classical economic system, competition was to be so perfect that no one person could have any substantial degree of power over others. Competition between businessmen was to keep prices close to costs, and wages close to the productive worth of employees. Competition among consumers, using their dollars as "votes for production," was to assure a balanced output of goods and services in the economy. In a really competitive system, such as classical economic theory envisaged, anyone trying to exploit anyone else would rapidly have found himself bid out of the economy by others. It was and is a nice picture.

The classical picture was spoiled, however, by the

introduction of innovation into the economy. New machinery, new lands, new kinds of organization, new products, new processes—the whole Schumpeterian array—made giant industry the most efficient institution for mass production and mass distribution. And with population rising rapidly, there could be little prospect of returning to less efficient small-scale methods in the mass-production areas of the economy. Giant industries, however, naturally accumulated giant powers over the rest of the community in every sphere of life, and those who controlled giant industry acquired power comparable to that of other ruling classes of the past. To meet this situation without either breaking up the giants or having them taken over by government, capitalism is experimenting with a system of countervailing power.

The principal author of the idea of countervailing power is John R. Commons (1862-1945), although it is Professor J. K. Galbraith to whom we owe the name and much of the theory.

Commons spent his life mainly as a professor of economics at the University of Wisconsin, but along the way he engaged in a great deal of economic research for various groups interested in social reforms. After his appointment at Wisconsin in 1904, he began work on various instruments of countervailing power. He helped draft a civil service bill to strengthen the professional side of government. He campaigned for municipal regulation of public utilities. He promoted a law limiting interest on small loans. He was a principal creator of the Wisconsin Industrial Commission, which was a forerunner of the many "alphabetical agencies" set up in the federal government by the New Deal. (It is not too much to say that Commons was the creator of the ideas and the techniques of the New Deal, which aimed to strengthen other groups in the economy in relation to the power of business.) Commons also wrote one of the first state unemployment insurance laws, and he was for twelve years (1923 to 1935) president of the National Consumers League. The reader who wishes to follow his important career more closely should read his autobiography, *Myself* (1934).

In his zeal for counterbalancing power (as he called it) Commons did not neglect his own profession. He was one of the founders of the American Association of University Professors. His account of this shows the nature of his motivation:

> Years afterwards, I joined with others of my teaching profession to form the American Association of University Professors, headed by the eminent Professor E. R. A. Seligman of the economics department at Columbia University. The purpose was to establish "academic freedom." I found that what was meant by academic freedom was exemption from the law of master and servant, so that we could have security of tenure and a hearing before dismissal. In one of the investigations made by the committee of the association, a member of the board of trustees of the university in question justified the removal of a professor by saying, "If I have a clerk in my store that I do not like, I fire him. These teachers are our employees. We drop them if we do not like them." He stated correctly the law of master and servant. But what the association of professors wanted was a hearing on the merits of each case of dismissal as to whether the dismissal would be justified in the interests of freedom to teach and speak. We wanted immunity from the common law of master and servant and named it "academic freedom." [1]

The other author of the theory of countervailing power is John Kenneth Galbraith (1909-), a professor of economics at Harvard. Professor Galbraith's career has been mainly as a teacher, but he has also had other professional experiences, as chief of price-control operations for the government during World War II, as an editor of *Fortune Magazine,* and as ambassador to India. His most popular book is *The Affluent Society* (1958), but for our purposes it should be read as a supplement to his earlier work, *American Capitalism: the Concept of Countervailing Power* (1952).

The new component of capitalism which countervailing power represents has already fulfilled, in the Western democracies, its promise of eliminating many ancient forms of tyranny. Such success is seldom achieved without costs, and we shall examine in the remainder of this chapter the new problems countervailing power has brought to the free economies. Assuming that there are solutions to be found for these problems, we shall note that the procedures of countervailing power have also opened up new vistas of hope for human beings, in terms of broader, more satisfying views of economic goals and economic tools, and more insight into the ways in which constructive economic activity can satisfy the human will.

The Bleeding Arm

One of the satisfactions of life as portrayed by the classical economists was the difficulty of making mistakes in bargaining about prices or wages. Under the completely competitive system (if it had ever existed), the merchant, the worker, and the consumer had only to ask what the going price or wage might be and accept it, since no one of them possessed a big enough share of the market to affect prices or wages by his own actions. Under a system of countervailing power, large organizations make large decisions (and possibly large mistakes), and the law of supply and demand has a different look.

Commons gives an interesting historical example of this new look as it operated in the achievement of the eight-hour day in the steel industry. The eight-hour day in steel was first proposed by management in 1889. Andrew Carnegie, one of the leading capitalists in the industry, had acquired patent rights for the continuous process of manufacturing steel, which required operation of the plant twenty-four hours a day. The employees were working a ten-hour day and Carnegie proposed a reduction to eight hours in three shifts rather than an increase to twelve with two shifts. The leaders of the union were strongly in favor of Carnegie's proposal, but it was voted down at the union's convention.

Carnegie apparently accepted this outcome, but three years later, in 1892, when H. C. Frick, Carnegie's partner, had come to power in the company, he eliminated the union at the Homestead plant by means not entirely peaceful, and installed the twelve-hour day and seven-day week for each employee with weekly changes from night shift to day shift for each worker, requiring twenty-four hours work on one Sunday and giving twenty-four hours off the next Sunday.

In 1907, Commons visited the Homestead plant and he has left us a description of an employee, a "heater" working under Frick's system:

> He was about fifty years of age, stripped to the waist, his left arm blistered and bloody from the heat of the oven. It was now eleven o'clock Sunday night. He had come to work that Sunday morning at six o'clock and would leave work at six o'clock the next morning. He had been on the day shift of twelve hours the preceding week and was then changing to the night shift of another

> twelve hours for the ensuing week. We saw the incredible. He talked freely to us as to friends during the intervals between opening and shutting the huge doors. Capable individuals, like Charles M. Schwab, had come out of that rugged individualism, but there were very few of them. This heater was an intelligent American citizen, not an immigrant pauper laborer. He was one of the high-paid wage earners.[2]

This situation went on, as Commons recounts it, until 1920, when the eight-hour day was installed by the steel company at the request of Republican campaign managers seeking votes in a political campaign. Then in 1935, it was solidified by an agreement with a newly-arisen industrial union.

Commons cites this series of incidents as an example of the way corporations, unions, and political parties control decisions under countervailing power. It also shows the importance of dominant personalities, as in the different policies of Carnegie and Frick, and it shows the importance of political processes within the countervailing organizations, as in the split between the leaders and the rank-and-file of the steelworkers' union in 1889. Had the employees accepted the union leaders' recommendations at that time, the eight-hour day would have been achieved in the steel industry thirty-one years earlier, in 1889 instead of in 1920.

The obvious lesson to be drawn is that the successful operation of a system of countervailing power requires leadership in all groups by men and women skilled in the long- and short-term strategy of their important decisions, and a constituency sufficiently educated to know when to back up the leadership. It is a very different world from the simple, powerless bargains contemplated in classical economic theory.

Widening the Goals

The theorists of countervailing power have sponsored another change in our thinking by suggesting that the goals of our economic system should be wider than the accumulation of more and more privately owned material goods and services. Thoughtful men and women have always known this, but it is sometimes not easy to get good sense into theory. No doubt the phrase "dismal science" so often applied to economics arose partly from the apparent overemphasis of economists of the nineteenth century upon the mere accumulation of goods.

By contrast, Commons says in his introduction to *The Economics of Collective Action:*

> If economic investigations are to implement the search of mankind for liberty, security, justice, equality or other great goals, it would seem that economists must analyze the political, economic and social relations by which these values are made available to, or secure for, the individual.[3]

And Galbraith begins *The Affluent Society* with a long-neglected quotation from Alfred Marshall, "The economist, like everyone else, must concern himself with the ultimate aims of man."

Galbraith has been especially insistent that we who live in the richer countries should recognize the disparity that exists between our private wealth and "public squalor." In the chapter called "The Theory of Social Balance" in *The Affluent Society,* he says that in all our cities we have overcrowded schools and hospitals, inadequate police protection, too few parks and playgrounds, filthy streets, slow public transport, and air dangerous to breathe.

The odd thing about this public poverty, Galbraith says,

is that it is increasing while private wealth is growing greater. In a famous passage from the same chapter, he says:

> The family which takes its mauve and cerise air-conditioned, power-steered and power-braked automobile out for a tour passes through cities that are badly paved, made hideous by litter, blighted buildings, billboards and posts for wires that should long since have been put underground. They pass on into a countryside that has been rendered largely invisible by commercial art. . . . They picnic on exquisitely packaged food from a portable icebox by a polluted stream and go on to spend the night in a park which is a menace to health and morals. Just before dozing off on an air mattress in a nylon tent, amid the stench of decaying refuse, they may reflect vaguely on the curious unevenness of their blessings. Is this, indeed, the American genius? [4]

There is very little satisfaction for the individual in our society even in the further growth of his private wealth, Galbraith says, because of "the dependence effect." This occurs when the satisfaction of our wants creates ever additional wants of equal or greater intensity. Our society often evaluates a person by the goods he possesses relatively to other persons, and so, the greater the general wealth of the economy, the more the individual wants to possess in order to maintain his status, whether or not he has any basic need for more possessions. His neighbor's new acquisition may be all that is necessary to create a new status-need in him, and there may be no end to keeping ahead of the Joneses. If his near neighbors do not create new needs in his mind, his far neighbors will oblige him in this respect through incessant advertising and salesmanship. And even those liberals who usually oppose great expenditures upon advertising as a source of waste in the economy may join in the cry for more unnecessary production in the name of creating more employment.

Galbraith's answer is that we should spend more to bring our public wealth into line with our private wealth.

Widening the Tools

Man is a tool-using animal. This has often been noted, and even described as man's distinctive trait. It would perhaps be truer to say that man is a tool-changing animal. Other forms of life—the bee, the beaver, and the bird, for example—build structures related to future production which may be described as tools, and a chimpanzee will pile up boxes and use a stick to knock down bananas, but these other forms of life seem to have no special tendency to improve their tools as time goes on, whereas throughout history some men have improved their tools with increasing frequency.

Man is also changing his concept of what tools are and what kinds of tools should be in the human tool kit and in what proportions. In *The Affluent Society,* Galbraith says, in a chapter called "The Investment Balance," that "investment in human beings is, prima facie, as important as investment in material capital," and he uses the term "personal capital" to describe investments in education.

During his stay in India as Ambassador from the United States, Galbraith wrote in *Foreign Affairs* magazine for April, 1961, in an article called "A Positive Approach to Economic Aid," that there are four tools essential to economic development:

1. Literacy for all and high skills for some, i.e., education.
2. Reliable public administration.
3. A good plan for development.
4. Social justice, i.e., a share in the fruits of economic development for all the people.

In this list, there is not only personal capital, regarded as a tool, as in the first item, but also social arrangements, as in the second item, plans, as in the third item, and even a goal—social justice—regarded as a tool, in the fourth item.

Other major economists have also been trying their hands at broadening our view of tools. One of them, Professor Theodore Schultz of the University of Chicago, said in his Presidential Address to the American Economic Association in 1960 that "human capital," as he called it, consists of training, health, and mobility, and he suggested that the rapid growth of the American economy in the past century is as much the result of the American willingness to invest in human capital as of its willingness to invest in material capital.

This line of thinking suggests that the theorists of countervailing power are preparing to try for a complete list of human tools as an advance upon the classical economic views of the subject. The classical economists used the word "capital" when they meant a tool, and they defined capital as "a produced means of further production," that is, something that we make not to eat or wear or enjoy watching, but to help us produce something consumable. The examples given in their books indicate that they thought of capital in the physical sense of roads, machines, buildings, and the like.

However, by adopting the word "capital" for "tool," the classical economists brought themselves into verbal conflict with businessmen who were using the term "capital" to mean the sum of money they were using in their business or holding ready for use at the first good opportunity. This conflict raised the question whether money is an economic tool. The Classicals were inclined to think not, taking the view that money is a veil behind which lie the real transactions with which economists must concern themselves. They spoke frequently of "the money veil."

Nevertheless, businessmen sensibly continued to maintain that money is a tool in the organization and operation of economic activity because of its power to arrange people into desired patterns of co-operation.

Money is a tool in a larger sense also, as an instrument helpful in managing the economy as a whole. We have seen, in discussing the Keynesian procedures for raising or lowering money-pressure in the economy, that substantial good can result from a proper modification of these pressures by various measures of control.

In a complete list of economic tools, therefore, we need to include *money* as well as the *physical capital* recognized by the classical economists.

Under the general heading of personal capital, we should include *health, skill,* and *motivation,* and we may add *mobility* to this group as well.

We can then set up, under the general heading of social capital, the kinds of arrangements which enable people to work together. The first of these is a group of *institutions,* including corporations, universities, courts, hospitals, co-operatives, government agencies, and the rest. The second is a group of *systems* in the economy, such as the banking system, the system of justice, the system of taxation, the system of collective bargaining, and others. (A system, in this sense, is a device for enabling institutions to work together.) And, as a last item under social capital, we should include *plans* as suggested by Galbraith.

In sum, our list of tools of man looks like this:

1. Money capital
2. Physical capital (roads, buildings, machinery, etc.)
3. Personal capital (health, skill, motivation, mobility)
4. Social capital (institutions, systems, plans)

One of the uses of such a list of tools is to moderate political discussions about poverty. Currently there are proposals to eliminate poverty in Appalachia in the southeastern quadrant of the United States, and lunch-table liberals are to be heard saying that education will do the trick, while the conservatives argue that new skills will not suffice because the people who are poor lack motivation to be other than they are.

By consulting our list of human tools, we may easily conclude that both education and motivation will be required in any poor area, and furthermore, that they will not be enough. Health and mobility will also have to be built up, as anyone knows who has tasted the Appalachian diet and has sensed the emotional comforts of a cabin in the laurels. And the other forms of capital will also have to be provided. Adequate physical capital either for farming or industry is almost absent in most of Appalachia. And social capital—the dozens of institutions, systems, and plans which affluence requires—are things of the future there. Our list of tools thus helps us to see the true dimensions of the job.

There is a similar use for the tool list in directing foreign aid. The United States has spent over a hundred billion dollars in helping other nations since 1945, and a great deal of the help has not been productive because it was not allocated according to any adequate list of what was needed. The first massive injections of aid were sent to Europe, and the response in terms of economic recovery was highly gratifying. This was because Europe was well equipped with all the forms of capital except for the physical capital destroyed in war, and the United States was well equipped to supply precisely this kind of capital.

Disappointment set in, however, when the same technique was applied to the underdeveloped nations, where all the forms of capital were inadequate. Tractors sent to one nation to increase food production could not be used satisfactorily because the landholding system provided for small strips of land on which the machines did not have adequate turning room. Water pumps sent to another nation became a problem because there was no wholesale-retail distribution network through which the right spare parts could be ordered, delivered, and fitted. Large sums sent to another nation went into the bank accounts of the rich and were soon transferred to their private accounts in Switzerland, because there was no system of honest public administration in that country. There were hundreds of such mistakes for lack of the use of an adequate list of the tools required and an adequate concept of a balance among the different kinds of tools.

Widening the Motives

Another result of using a countervailing power component in the capitalist system is to require economists to consider a wider range of economic motives than the classical economists thought necessary. To Smith, Mill, Marshall, and their classical colleagues it seemed sufficient to suppose that Economic Man sought to maximize the difference between pleasure and pain. For the merchant, this meant maximizing his profit; for the consumer, maximizing the utilities received from goods and services; and, for the worker, maximizing the net returns from his efforts. These economists did not suppose that there was nothing more to man's mind and spirit than a "min-max" computer, but since they were considering only an individualistically competitive group of decision makers, the assumption seemed to them worthwhile. One of its values was that it could easily be translated into mathematical terms.

When we come to the procedures of countervailing power, the assumption must be different because many collective economic decisions are being made by many different kinds of groups. Labor unions, scientific organizations, government agencies, legal and medical groups, organized churches, schools and colleges, and many other groups make decisions not primarily based on the profit motive in the classical sense. And these organizations include individuals with the widest range of personal motives for their activities, from the deep devotion of some scientists, teachers, and religious leaders to the grossest short-term profit seeking of some used car dealers, funeral directors, and "home-improvement" salesmen.

There are thoughtful people who will argue that even the devoted person is selfishly pursuing his own happiness which just happens to spring from devotion to the welfare of others, but even if this point of view is accepted, we are still left with a valid distinction between the direct selfishness of some and the indirect selfishness of others. Indirect selfishness has the advantage to society of satisfying itself by way of aiding others, in contrast to direct selfishness which simply takes from others what it has the power to take.

To cope with these considerations, Commons proposed to make the human will the basic motive force in economic theory. In his *Legal Foundations of Capitalism* (1924), he writes:

> The will is always up against something. It is always performing, avoiding, forbearing, that is, always moving along lines, not of least resistance like physical forces without purpose, but of overcoming resistance . . . with a purpose looking toward the future.[5]

And, in the *Economics of Collective Action,* Commons writes that economic decisions are reducible to four dimensions of the will in action—performance, forbearance, avoidance, and timeliness:

> Performance is the 100 per cent positive act of self to the full extent of one's ability without any external command or restraint whatever. Forbearance is self-restraint, ranging in all degrees of power over self from zero restraint, or liberty, up to avoidance which is 100 per cent self-restraint in that direction. And avoidance is therefore choice of the next best alternative performance—not free will, which is subjective, but free choice which is objective and measurable. Timing or timeliness, or the selection of the right time, right place, and right degree of power, is the fourth of the space-time dimensions of self-command.[6]

One advantage of using the human will instead of the classical min-max assumption is that the min-max assumption can also be included in Commons' basic term. Where it is the will of businessmen simply to maximize their profits or minimize their losses, or where it is the will of consumers to maximize their utilities or of workers to minimize their sacrifices, these can be looked upon as special cases of the will in action. The use of will as the basic drive also permits economics to link up with discoveries in psychology about the variety of drives and stresses that make the will what it is.

Commons remarked about will that it is the only force in nature, as far as we know, which can restrain its own action. The lightning in the summer storm flashes with its fullest force, and the flood sloshes over the town without any thought of moderation, but the will can forbear.

Forbearance

The theory and practice of forbearance becomes of crucial importance in the use of a countervailing power procedure under capitalism, because the organized groups are so powerful that the exertion of full power by any one of them over an extended period could cripple the economy. Organized farmers have the power to deprive the nation of food. Organized labor can disrupt the production and transport of goods. Organized government can tyrannize over everybody. Organized industry, like organized labor, can stop production and the improvement of production. (See Ayn Rand's novel, *Atlas Shrugged*, for an imaginative picture of a full-scale strike by industrialists.) Even the organized professions, when they use all their power, can cause great difficulty, as recent strikes by doctors in Canada and Belgium have shown.

The theorists of countervailing power have themselves warned against the overpursuit of power. In *American Capitalism*, Galbraith writes:

> There remains, of course, the chance that power, developed and even encouraged to neutralize other power, will start on a career of its own. This is the spectre which has been raised by nearly every critic of the concept of countervailing power, even the friendliest ones. The danger may exist. No one can tell. It is some comfort that those who have worked most cohesively to develop countervailing power—the unions and the major farm organizations in particular—have so far comported themselves with some restraint. This is an area, we need remind ourselves, where anything that is novel has an unparalleled aspect of danger. Economic power, even in its most elementary form, evokes such fears.[7]

The absolutely prime forbearance needed is that no one of the organized groups should aspire to complete power over the economy, and all groups should be prepared to unite to stop any attempt of one group to take over. The basic idea of countervailing power is that no group of people has divine right or ideological right to exclusive rule. In the past, great trouble has been taken to oust priests, generals, landowners, industrialists, and others who at certain times and places claimed primacy.

Nowadays, the fear seems to be that governmental executives themselves, with self-perpetuating power, as in Communist countries, may become the chief threat to the system of countervailing power through the theory that the "State" is sacred.

To counteract any such tendency, Commons defines the State as simply "the collective action of politicians." In *The Economics of Collective Action,* he describes his attempt to introduce unionism into government service in Wisconsin:

> At first I failed when I tried to introduce it [collective bargaining] into the civil service law of the state in 1905. The legislature was then alarmed at the suggestion of collective action by employees of so sacred an organization as "the State." But since that time the employees of the state government, that is, the employees of the politicians, have effected an organization on their own initiative, and have even obtained a considerable amount of recognition by the politicians in modifying the working rules of the civil service of the state. It turns out that "the State" was the collective action of politicians. The three principal kinds of collective action in the twentieth century are corporations, labor unions, and political parties.[8]

And again, in discussing his insistence that accident-prevention programs should be transferred from the state of Wisconsin to private insurance companies able to handle them effectively, Commons speaks of the importance of withdrawing functions from the state when voluntary associations can do them as well or better. He writes:

> Most of all, it requires putting over the idea of a new kind of government. Lawyers, judges and politicians are

instinctively opposed to it. They have the traditional idea of government as a coercive power from above, imposing laws and inflicting punishments on those subject to their authority. But if we look at government as it actually operates, what is government? What is the State of Wisconsin? What is the United States of America? It is the political parties that elect the legislators and judges and appoint the hundreds of deputies, inspectors, statisticians and clerks who administer the laws. . . . But we must learn to keep party politics (i.e., government) within the field where needed so that voluntary associations can operate in the field where they can be effective.[9]

Modern conservatives welcome this "de-sacredizing" of government in the procedure of countervailing power, even though, as the principal holders of original power, they suffer irritation from the "impudence" of organizations among formerly weaker groups. Galbraith tries to console these conservatives with the thought that "set against the loss of their authority is their greater prospect for an agreeable old age."[10]

Commons' view of democracy, he tells us in *Myself,* is not the historic meaning of a majority overruling a minority, but "representation of organized, voluntary but conflicting economic interests" in an "organized equilibrium of equality." The essential point, he says, is the elimination of a third party, whether king, legislature, governor or dictator, handing down rules and regulations from above—and the substitution of rules agreed upon collectively by conciliation.[11]

Reason

If we are to ask the organized groups of our society not to exercise their full powers, and not to accept any one group as sacred, in what name and to what extent shall we ask them to forbear and conciliate with one another? Commons' answer was that the groups should accept reason as their guide. And he recommended a specific technique for determining what reasonableness would be in particular cases, realizing that the usual criticism of reason as a criterion is that there are as many ideas of reason as there are individuals. He also wanted to avoid the view, often accepted by courts, that reason is the average of existing practices. He was as much interested in avoiding stagnation as in avoiding anarchy.

Commons defined reason as "idealism limited by practicability," that is, as the highest standards of practice that the particular situation would permit. In the field of labor standards in which he did most of his work, Commons favored, on each issue that arose, a committee composed of high-ranking representatives of the conflicting parties to find out what were the prevailing practices of the more progressive employers, and then to recommend bringing the other employers up to that standard. Thus "existing best practices" became the goal of reason.[12]

As an example of one of his early "works" in the practice of countervailing power, Commons mentions the committee on boiler safety of the Industrial Commission of Wisconsin. It was his responsibility to initiate the committee, and he appointed to it a manufacturer of boilers, a manufacturer who used boilers, an insurance company's inspector of boilers, an employee who operated boilers, and a steam locomotive engineer. This committee, paid nothing but its expenses, devoted much of its spare time for a year to investigating best practices and average practices in the field of boiler safety, and arrived at a code for the subject which, after a public hearing, was issued by the Industrial Commission as an order applying to all makers and users of boilers.

Commons was proud of the fact that the courts accepted such codes as reasonable. "Reasonableness," he writes, "was now deemed to be ascertained, not by conflicting agreements and pleadings in court or legislature, nor by legal precedents, nor by ordinary custom, nor by opinions of judges, but by collective action of leading representatives of conflicting interests."[13]

One thing that can go wrong with these collective agreements is collusive action by two or more interested groups against the interests of other groups which are represented only weakly, if at all. Galbraith has been extremely critical of a particular example of this, which he calls the collusion of organized industry and organized labor in creating the upward wage-price spiral so familiar to us in times of inflation. He goes so far as to say that a substantial percentage of unemployment is desirable if it is required to discourage such collusion.

Arbitrators

A special feature of the countervailing-power component is its development of a corps of arbitrators. The term arbitrator is reserved in law for a person who acts as an impartial judge in an economic dispute. It is distinguished from the term "mediator" or "conciliator," who makes suggestions and tries to bring the conflicting parties closer together, but whose conclusions are not legally binding as are an arbitrator's.

A system of arbitration arises for several good reasons. One is that the groups whose powers countervail one another do not always wish to test their economic strength on every matter that comes up. It is convenient for the groups themselves to toss a host of relatively small issues into the laps of impartial experts who will render workable decisions about them. Another reason is the feeling which grows as society progresses that settlement of issues on the basis of strength is not always desirable. There should be an element of justice, based upon developed ideas of what is fair, applied to the facts of the dispute as established by hearing and investigation. Sometimes there is a strategic consideration when a dispute is sent to arbitration. One party or the other may actually wish to give in, but its executives, fearing a loss of face, may prefer to let an arbitrator tell them they have a poor case rather than admit it themselves.

There are several special features of arbitration which are designed to make it practical for settling economic disputes when decisions obtained through the courts would be too slow, too expensive, and too legalistic. For one thing, in the United States, the conflicting parties must agree upon the person who is to be the arbitrator of their dispute. They can agree directly upon someone, or they may ask for a panel of names from the Federal Mediation and Conciliation Service in Washington for labor-management disputes, or from the numerous offices of a private, non-profit organization, the American Arbitration Association, for all types of disputes.

Selection of an arbitrator from a panel of, say, five names, is often made by flipping a coin to see which of the disputing parties may first strike off two of the names. Then the other party may strike two names. The remaining person is the arbitrator. Another method is to have each party number the five arbitrators in order of preference and then, after combining the scores, to select as arbitrator the person with the lowest number. In rare cases, the parties agree upon some respected person in the community to select their arbitrator, but in one way or another they have to do it themselves, instead of having a judge assigned to them as in a regular court.

Once the parties appear before an arbitrator, other differences from the procedures of courts occur. The hearing is relatively informal and the final decision is rendered within a few weeks instead of months or years later. Opportunities for appeal from an arbitration decision are almost non-existent. The regular courts will accept such appeals only if there are defects in the procedures of the arbitration. Procedural requirements, usually set down in state statutes of arbitration, are notably simple, and it is refreshing that cases before arbitrators are almost never won or lost by the technicalities and surprises that much oftener prevail in courts. Arbitrators are not bound by precedent, as courts are, nor are they bound entirely by what they hear in the hearing room. They can and do frequently leave the hearing, in the company of representatives of the parties, to investigate the facts and circumstances of a dispute on the site itself. Also, since arbitrators can apply a wider variety of criteria in reaching their decisions, the results can be more satisfying to the parties than the usual legal decisions.

In 1960, the United States Supreme Court issued three decisions which officially recognized the arbitrators of labor-management disputes as part of the judicial system of the nation. It happens that the arbitration of labor-management disputes is more advanced than the arbitration of disputes between other countervailing interests, but it seems likely that arbitration of disputes between the other interests will, in due course, be given equal recognition. The arbitrators of labor-management disputes are organized as a profession into the National Academy of Arbitrators, and the annual proceedings of the Academy, published in yearly volumes, are the best material for the reader who would like to know more about this subject.

Organization Man

Life teaches us that nearly every asset has its costs, and one of the costs of using countervailing power as a component of capitalism is the loss, at least partially, of the classical economists' ideal of man. They thought the world of their own time was overorganized, especially for repressive purposes, and they looked forward to a future in which each individual would stand on his own feet and make his own decisions and think his own thoughts.

The world we live in, however, imposes a different requirement. As Commons put it:

> This is an age of collective action. Most Americans must work collectively as participants in organized concerns in order to earn a living. In this collective process, persons engage in collective bargaining, for in this way individual wills meet and become part of the collective will.[14]

In his popular book, *The Organization Man* (1956), William H. Whyte, Jr. expressed the fears and discontents of many over the degradation of people engaged in "collective willing." Whyte deplored the loss of individuality, the excessive number of team projects, committee meetings, and large conferences, and the forced adjustment of the individual to the group. Among business executives he saw this bleak conformity reaching even into the hours after work, blighting the standardized suburbs with forced "togetherness" in open-plan houses where there was no privacy and where "filiarchy" (rule by children) prevailed.

Whyte did say that organized work need not always be

subject to these evils. He found a few corporations whose research laboratories encouraged scientists to work as individuals, and a few individuals with courage to rebel against the arbitrary powers of their organizations, but Whyte's outlook was pessimistic, and the long waiting list for his book at public libraries, as well as its position on best-seller lists, indicated the extent of public apprehension about the new kind of man being molded by countervailing organizations.

Commons took a more optimistic view of the possibilities open to organization men. "Collective action," he wrote, "means more than mere control of individual action. It means liberation and expansion of individual action; thus collective action is literally the means to liberty."[15] In contrast to Whyte's views, Commons felt that the modern corporation liberated the individual by permitting him to develop specialized abilities and to receive help from other specialists, with the result that his performance and his standard of living were much higher than if he were running some small enterprise by himself.

Commons did recognize, however, that the organizations of a countervailing-power society will not automatically behave well toward their members. On the contrary, an organization purporting to protect and advance the individual may itself become a tyranny over him. One might say that a countervailing-power society, in order to avoid central tyranny, distributes power among a number of "private governments." There is then the problem of getting those smaller governments to serve the interests of individuals and individualism.

Commons' view was that society must impose duties upon organizations to behave well toward their members. These duties could be self-imposed through voluntarily adopted codes, or failing that, they could be imposed by law. The object of the code or law is to make each individual "a citizen of the concern," and "a center of discretion and influence," to use Commons' terms. The properly organized corporations, Commons said, work through general rules which require them to treat all individuals alike, regardless of personal likes and dislikes, using an adequate merit system. Such at least is the ideal of the theory of countervailing power, and it was against departures from the ideal, especially in relation to corporation executives, that Whyte was protesting in *The Organization Man*.

Summary

The component of countervailing power has been introduced into capitalism to solve the age-old problem of great economic power and its ever faithful companion, the oppression of the powerless. As soon as it became obvious in modern life that provision for the increasing masses of humanity required mass production by enormous enterprises with enormous power, two economic theorists, John Rogers Commons and John Kenneth Galbraith, began to work out a theory of the control of the economy by organizations representing the main economic interests which co-operate in production and are in partial conflict about the conditions of production and the division of the fruits. As a result of the work of these theorists, we understand a great deal about the proper role in the economy of organized industry, organized labor, organized science, organized religion, organized education, organized agriculture, and all other groups organized or to be organized, including consumers, the aged, the unemployed, and others.

Yet, if mankind has at last conquered the fact of oppression by powerful minorities—whether landowners, priests, industrialists, militarists, bureaucracies, proletarians, or others—we know already that to keep this priceless advantage we must pay a great price in new ways of thinking. In classical economic theory, it was comforting to think that no individual, as consumer or worker or businessman, could make a huge economic mistake involving others. In an economy of countervailing power, where giant organizations bargain together, immense strategic mistakes involving thousands, even millions, of others may be made by wrong judgment, however well-intentioned. And no longer may anyone in our economic society urge his group to the exercise of its maximum power. To keep the necessary balances we must practice forbearance and walk in the paths of reason, and, at suitable times, submit vital issues to the decision of expert, impartial arbitrators.

In another direction, the theory of countervailing power stretches our minds to think what it is that men and women are really shopping for in life—what goods, what freedoms, what environments, what forms of security, what developments of personality? And the theory seeks to broaden our views of the tools and the justifiable motives we may bring into play in achieving these desires.

A substantial accomplishment of the theorists of countervailing power is thus to have put economics in touch again with other disciplines which discuss the meaning of the good life—especially religion, philosophy, and psychology. When someone accused Commons of trying to destroy capitalism, he answered, "I was trying to save capitalism by making it good."[16]

CHAPTER 6

Wanting What's Good for Us: the element of stimulation

The last of our five components of a free economy is stimulation—the psychological impetus in individuals urging them on to create a satisfying standard of living. Those who live in the affluent societies of the world are inclined to take this element of capitalism for granted and to think it odd or sinful that a minority in their midst seem to be without economic ambition. But as we look back into history we see, as Arnold Toynbee put it in *A Study of History* (1933), that out of some 900 human societies of which some trace has been found, only about 30, as Toynbee classifies them, have ever pulled themselves out of the mud and dust to achieve a fairly comfortable life for any substantial number of their citizens. Therefore, we must not suppose that there is anything "natural" or inborn about economic initiative. It has to be created within the individual as an energizing philosophy of life.

Historic ruins around the world tell us also that the will to economic progress has to be maintained or it will slip away. Toynbee notes that of the thirty civilizations which achieved a degree of prosperity, all but five (again using his classification) have gone under. It is one of the curiosities of modern life that the affluence of individuals often shows itself in trips abroad to inspect the ruined remains of once powerful economies. Perhaps the more thoughtful of the tourists hope that among the tumbled stones and broken columns there will appear a cautionary message about the means of maintaining our own economic growth.

Economists are much less secure in their reasoning about stimulation than about the other essential procedures of capitalism. It is only recently, as the wealthier nations have sought to help the whole world to raise itself to a higher level of prosperity, that the full importance and difficulty of stimulating humanity have become evident.

The Prosperity Ethic

A few decades ago, a number of economists noticed that the most properous nations in the world in the twentieth century have been predominantly Protestant Christian in religious belief (with a substantial number of Jews in their urban centers). It has become common among economists to call the stimulating economic views of this religion the "Protestant Ethic." Thus far in human history, the Protestant Ethic has been very much the most potent economic stimulator the world has ever seen, and we shall examine it in some detail.

However, we shall not be led to the conclusion that the world must be Protestant to be prosperous, since not all of the Protestant world is stimulated (Appalachia is one example) and since there are stimulating ideas similar to the Protestant Ethic in other prominent religions and philosophies. Just as the Protestant Ethic arose in a reformation of the Christian religion, so a similar ethic is being developed in reformations in other religions. And in some religions which have had stimulating effects in the past and have since lost them, there are attempts being made to recover what has been lost.

As a result, we shall use the term "Prosperity Ethic" to refer to the economically stimulating views in each religion or philosophy of life and leave the term "Protestant Ethic" to its own area. The truth is that there are pro-prosperity views and anti-prosperity views in every known religion, although at any one time either the pro- or the anti-view may predominate.

IN PROTESTANTISM. The Prosperity Ethic brought into Christianity by Luther and Calvin during the sixteenth century A.D. consists of six doctrines which may be summarized as follows:

1. *The two kingdoms.* Religion requires us to participate in earthly activities, enjoying the fruits of the earth and performing its duties while recognizing that we are on earth only temporarily as guests. We must therefore use the world without abusing it. This doctrine avoids two extremes, the one of living only for salvation in the after-life and the other of living selfishly and heedlessly to maximize personal pleasure in this life.

2. *Vocation.* All honest work is sacred if done well and with a sense of service to others. This replaces the older view that only certain holy vocations in religious service are sacred and that ordinary work is a curse put upon mankind as a punishment for sin. Far from being a curse, the Protestant Ethic says, ordinary everyday work is

essential and natural and pleasing to God and we must continue it to our last days.

3. *Profits and service.* This doctrine says that the business-man should not sell his goods at the highest possible price but should honor his sacred obligation to help the buyer, and should seek profits only from his own energy and diligence in serving the buyer. This is intended to replace the extreme views (a) that any kind of rapacity is justified in business if it maximizes profits and (b) that any kind of profit-making is somehow immoral, sordid, and anti-spiritual.

4. *Wealth.* Riches, honestly made, are acceptable if they are regarded by the rich as held in stewardship by them to be spent or invested for the benefit of their fellow men. This is intended to replace the old anti-prosperity doctrine that it is harder for a rich man to enter the kingdom of heaven than for a camel to pass through the eye of a needle. To be acceptable to God, the rich need not give all they have to the poor, but simply use it wisely and accountably for the general good.

5. *Science.* Science, defined as inquiry and knowledge, is naturally an independent province of human activity and the Church should have no jurisdiction over it.

6. *Taxation.* Rulers must take from their subjects only what is necessary to supply the common needs of the people so that private citizens can accumulate capital. This replaces the extreme doctrine that the whole surplus above subsistence belongs to the ruler to be spent on his own splendor and glory, and also another extreme doctrine in many underdeveloped nations that little or no taxation shall be laid upon the rich to pay for common needs.

In view of the impact these doctrines have had upon our economic life, it is interesting to hear the words of Luther and Calvin themselves as they made these revolutionary changes in religious doctrine upon which is built the prosperity of the great arc of predominantly Protestant nations stretching from Finland westward to New Zealand. It is not too much to say that only insofar as these same attitudes and ideals are uncovered and made predominant in other major religions and philosophies of life will it be practical to hope for world prosperity.

Luther begins his economic theory by prescribing a balance between our participation in the joys and duties of this world and our regard for the next. In *A Treatise on Christian Liberty* (1520), he says:

> Christians are subjects of two kingdoms—they have experience of two kinds of life. Here on earth where the world has its home and its heavenly kingdom, we surely are not citizens. . . . But being obliged to continue in this wretched state—our Babylon—so long as God wills, we should do as the Jews were commanded to do—mingle with other mortals, eat and drink, make homes, till the soil, fill civil offices and show good will toward our fellows, even praying for them, until the hour arrives for us to depart unto our home. In short, a Christian must be one who as Paul says (I Corinthians 7, 29-31) uses this world without abusing it. . . . The Christian's attitude toward this earthly life is the attitude of the guest; that in such capacity is he to build, to buy, to have dealings and hold intercourse with his fellows, to join them in all temporal affairs—a guest who respects his host's wishes, the laws of the realm and of the city and the customs of the inn, but at the same time the Christian refrains from attesting his satisfaction with this life as if he intended to remain here and hoped for nothing better.[1]

This is the key quotation for all of Luther's contribution to the Protestant Ethic. In it we have his emphasis on enjoyable consumption of worldly goods instead of rejection of the world and acceptance of suffering as the means to salvation, beliefs which were characteristic of the Middle Ages in Europe. We also have the exhortation to work and to accept civic duties instead of aspiring to a life of meditation and prayer or of lordly leisure. Yet Luther urges us to forbearance in our use of the world since we are guests here and not owners.

Luther was critical of the passive acceptance of poverty and of the view that we need to do nothing to modify reality since the Lord will provide. Referring to the well-known Biblical passage about taking no thought for the morrow, he writes in his *Treatise on Good Works* (1520):

> Yes, rely upon that, take no thought, and see whether a roasted chicken will fly into your mouth. I do not say that a man should not labor and seek a living; but he shall not worry, not be greedy, not despair, thinking that he will not have enough, for in Adam we are all condemned to labor when God says to him, "In the sweat of thy face shalt thou eat bread." And in Job, "As the bird to flying, so is man born to labor." Now the birds fly without worry and greed; and so we also should labor without worry and greed, but if you do worry and are greedy, wishing that the roasted chicken fly into your mouth: worry and be greedy and see whether you will thereby fulfill God's Commandment and be saved! [2]

The people of the Protestant nations are so familiar with these ideas about work that they may find it hard to imagine what a change Luther had made in the medieval view that work was a mark of lowliness and a kind of curse from which all worthy people sought to escape either into a holy vocation or a knightly life of war, women, and song.

In his *Epistle Sermons,* Luther hammered home the thought that all work is sacred:

> Since it is God's will that everyone should serve his fellows here in his respective station, in the office committed to him, we shall do whatever is enjoined upon us. We will serve our subjects, our neighbors, our wives and children so long as we can; we would not relax our service even if we knew we had to depart this very hour and leave all earthly things.[3]

Luther accorded businessmen an esteem withheld from them by the medieval Church, but he insisted that they practice forbearance and make their profits through service to others. In his essay "On Trading and Usury" (1524) he writes:

> The merchants have among themselves one common rule which is their chief maxim and the basis of all their sharp practices. They say: I may sell my goods as dear as I can. This they think their right. But that is giving way to avarice and opening every door and window to hell. . . . For your selling ought not be a work that is within your own power and will without law or limit, as though you were a god and beholden to no one; but because this selling of yours is a work that you perform toward your neighbor, it must be so governed by law and conscience that you do it without harm and injury to your neighbor.[4]

This doctrine is the same as Adam Smith's "enlightened self-interest," or Commons' forbearance, or "indirect selfishness," as we have called it. It seeks to take advantage of the immense energies liberated by selfish pursuits but to channel them within limits of law and forbearance so that the individual benefits himself through benefiting others.

Luther was correct in supposing that these doctrines of worldly enjoyment without abuse, of lifelong work as a sacred duty, and of enlightened selfishness in business would produce economic progress. He was fully aware, also, that the gains could be thrown away unless taxation and spending by government were guided by new ideas. The custom in his time was for rulers to assess how much each family would need to keep to get through the year and confiscate the rest to be spent on the ruler's power and glory.

Luther had a different idea. In his *Admonition to Peace, A Reply to the Twelve Articles of the Peasants in Swabia* (1525), he says:

> Rulers are not instituted in order that they may seek their own profit and self-will, but in order to provide for the best interests of their subjects. Flaying and extortion are, in the long run, intolerable. What good would it do if a peasant's field bore as many gold coins as stalks or grains of wheat if that only meant the ruler would take all the more and make his splendor all the greater and squander the property on clothing, eating, drinking, building and the like, as though it were chaff? The splendor would have to be checked and the expenditure stopped so that a poor man could keep something.[5]

This forbearance by government is, of course, an essential foundation of the almost innumerable accumulations of private capital upon which, among other things, a free economy is based.

In only two matters was Luther opposed to the complete prosperity ethic as we know it today. He was quite distrustful of the movement of the economy from the predominance of agriculture to the predominance of industry which is a step on the way to prosperity. He wrote in *An Open Letter to the Christian Nobility* (1520): "This I know well, that it would be much more pleasing to God if we increased agriculture and diminished commerce."[6]

Nor could Luther find a functional place for the very

rich in his idea of the economic system. In the *Letter* just mentioned, he speaks of the richest family of his own day: "We must put a bit in the mouth of the Fuggers and similar corporations. How is it possible that in the lifetime of a single man such great possessions, worthy of a king, can be piled up and yet everything be done legally and according to God's will?"[7]

When Calvin worked out his supplement to Luther's economic ethic, he found a place for the rich through the idea of stewardship. Not asking them to give their wealth to the poor, nor putting them aside as condemned, Calvin wrote in his *Institutes of the Christian Religion* (1559):

> There cannot be imagined a more certain rule, or a more powerful exhortation to the observance of it, than when we are taught that all the blessings we enjoy are Divine deposits committed to our trust on this condition: that they should be dispensed for the benefit of our neighbors. . . . Whatever God has conferred upon us which enables us to assist our neighbor, we are the stewards of it and must one day render an account of our stewardship; and the only right dispensation of what has been committed to us is that which is regulated by the law of love.[8]

In conformance with this doctrine, we find that most of the Protestant nations of the world have been willing to let the rich keep most of their wealth, and in return the rich, instead of building enormous palaces and private armies, have invested their money in enterprises which make goods and services for the people. It was a substantial help to this idea when Schumpeter defined the role of the rich more precisely as investors in innovation. Innovation is so deeply essential, especially when population is expanding rapidly, that the rich now have outlined for them a specific and secure economic function. In the Protestant nations, the rich have, generally speaking, accepted this function. Whether the rich of other faiths and other lands will do so remains a very vital question.

Calvin also encouraged the growth of industry provided that its profits were made by "energy, diligence and industry" and not by "rushing forward to seize wealth or honors, by unlawful actions, by deceitful and criminal acts, by rapacity and injury to our neighbors."[9] Calvin set the example by introducing two industries into Switzerland —watchmaking and textile manufacture.

Calvin also saw the importance of science and accepted the necessity of its independence from religious control. "Faith," he wrote, "consists not in ignorance but in knowledge and that not only of God but of the Divine Will. For we do not obtain salvation by our promptitude to embrace as truth whatever the Church may have prescribed, or by our transferring to her the province of inquiry and knowledge."[10]

Concerning the importance to the economy of restraint in government spending, Calvin was at least as emphatic as Luther. Princes, he said, must remember that their revenues are not their own to squander as they please, but "are to be considered as the blood of the people, not to spare which is the most inhuman cruelty, and their various imposts and tributes ought to be regarded merely as aids to the public necessity, to burden the people with which, without cause, would be tyrannical rapacity."[11]

Calvin added a special meaning to Luther's doctrine of salvation through faithful work in one's own calling. He said that eternal life in heaven is not a reward for work, but rather, success in work is a sign that the successful person is preordained for salvation. To the mind of God, Calvin said, all events whether past, present, or future are known.

He knows, therefore, who will be saved and who will be damned, but the only way by which a human being can know that he will be saved is by success in his vocation.

For Calvin as for Luther, success could be achieved in any honest and useful work. As Calvin put it, "There will be no employment so mean and sordid, provided we follow our vocation, as not to appear truly respectable and be deemed highly important in the sight of God."[12]

It is tempting at this point to recount the growth of economic ideas similar to those of Luther and Calvin in other religions of the Western world—Roman Catholicism, Eastern Orthodox Christianity, Judaism, and Humanism, but that would take more space than we have in this book and must be left to another valume. What we can do here is to give several illustrations of the development of a Prosperity Ethic in other religions of the world.

IN ISLAM. One of the most interesting and important examples is Islam, the religion of the Moslems. It is interesting because it shows us a religion which started with an effective Prosperity Ethic and then lost it and is now trying to find it again. And it is important because of the vast area, population, and resources of the Islamic world.

Today, the Moslem civilization, containing one-fifth of humanity, is a vast area of poverty extending from Dakar on the Atlantic coast of Africa eastward across North Africa and the Middle East to Afghanistan and Pakistan in Asia. Yet at one time this was the strongest, richest, and most learned empire on earth. The standard of living which the Moslems achieved from the seventh to the twelfth century A.D. was not attained in Europe until the sixteenth and seventeenth centuries. And the free-trade area which the Moslems organized from China to Spain and from Russia to central Africa has never been equalled before or since. In the golden age of their empire from 900 to 1100 A.D.,

Moslems led the world by a long way in medicine, physics, chemistry, astronomy, mathematics, geography, and architecture.

There was sufficient economic stimulation in Mohammed's doctrines to create and sustain the great period of prosperity in Islam. A few brief quotations from his religious sayings will show the trend of his economic thought.

> The Son of Man grows and with him grow two things—the love of wealth and the love of long life.
>
> It is better to teach knowledge one hour in the night than to pray the whole night.
>
> The ink of the scholar is more holy than the blood of the martyr.
>
> One learned man is harder on the devil than a thousand ignorant worshippers.
>
> Who are the learned? They who practice what they know.
>
> Whoever bringeth the dead land to life, for him is reward therein.
>
> No man is a true believer unless he desireth for his brother that which he desireth for himself.
>
> Charity is a duty unto every Moslem.
>
> Doing justice between two people is charity, and assisting a man upon his beast and lifting his baggage is charity; and pure comforting words are charity and answering questions with mildness is charity; and removing that which is an inconvenience to wayfarers such as thorns and stones is charity.
>
> Woe to the miser who blocks up the channels of use and service and dams up his wealth.
>
> I and the man who brings up an orphan will be in Paradise together.

> There are three persons whose adversary in dispute I shall be on the day of Resurrection; a person who makes a promise in my name and then acts unfaithfully; a person who sells a free person and then devours the price; and a person who employs a servant and receives fully the labor due from him and then does not pay his wage.[13]

These are all pro-prosperity teachings—pro-science, pro-education, pro-investment, pro-activism, and favorable to reliable and co-operative economic activities. Why, then, are so many Moslem nations underdeveloped today?

Unfortunately, an anti-prosperity reformation occurred in Islam just prior to the beginning of its economic decline. It was the work of Abu Hamal al-Ghazali (1059-1111), of whom it is usually said that if there could be two prophets of Islam, he would be the second. Al-Ghazali was educated as a lawyer and a theologian and was a professor of divinity who had achieved honor and success when, at the age of 37, he had a sudden conversion. His whole life and all its worldly concerns suddenly appeared to him as worthless in view of the eternal life after death, and he abandoned his position, his family, and his friends and devoted the rest of his life to writing and preaching that pro-prosperity activities were evil and could only lead the individual to eternal suffering in hellfire.

In his massive book, *The Revival of Religious Knowledge,* al-Ghazali lists the possession of worldly goods and the pursuit of wealth as deadly sins. Poverty, he says, is essential to eternal salvation. And religious duty does not consist of the economic activities commended by Mohammed, but rather of five ceremonial and ritual acts—prayer, purification, almsgiving, pilgrimage, and reciting the Koran.

As for the splendid structure of Islamic science, al-Ghazali declared it blasphemous and recommended that it be dismantled completely, and this was done in succeeding generations as his teachings became dominant in Islam. The basic idea of science, that there are reliable connections between events in the world, was cast aside by al-Ghazali as unholy, a denial of God's omnipotence. He wrote that God is the only possible cause of connection between any two events and God cannot be constrained to make things happen always in the same sequence. According to this anti-scientific theory, which bears the impressive name of "Islamic occasionalism," the only source of our understanding of the universe is in the words of mystic holy men.[14]

In spite of al-Ghazali, the relative prosperity of the Moslem empire continued for another five centuries, primarily because the economic enthusiasm created by Mohammed shifted to places where al-Ghazali's ideas had not become dominant. During Mohammed's lifetime, most of Arabia had been converted to Islam and the stimulation became greatest in Syria with Damascus as its capital. A century later, the center of stimulation had shifted to the Persians and the capital of Islam was moved to the newly-built city of Bagdad. Later, the capitals became plural, one at Cordova in Spain and one at Cairo in Egypt, in addition to Bagdad. After a few centuries more, economic leadership within the empire shifted again, first to the Seljuk Turks who had originally come in from Asia and secured employment as mercenary soldiers, and then to the Ottoman Turks, also from central Asia, who seized Constantinople in 1453, and were denied possession of Europe only by their defeat at Vienna in 1683.

By the sixteenth century, however, the Ghazalian economic ethic had become prominent even in the Ottoman section of the Moslem area. As H. A. R. Gibb and Harold Bowen have shown in the informative volumes of their *Islamic Society and the West* (1950 and 1958), the apathy and resignation that took over Islamic society occurred from top to bottom. The sultans retired into the seclusion of palace life, giving up their former functions of encouraging learning and of maintaining their palaces as centers of stimulation. The apparatus of science and education was dismantled. Official positions in the empire, both civil and religious, became hereditary instead of being constantly refreshed by able persons from each new generation. The learned professions—law, medicine, teaching, and others—simply decayed. Thus did the Moslem empire lose its former prosperity ethic and settle back into the view that the main duty of man is to perform requisite rituals and ceremonies in hope of a good life after death.

There is some evidence that the present leaders of the Arab world recognize the need for a reformation in Islam to recreate the original prosperity ethic of Mohammed. In his book, *Egypt's Liberation—The Philosophy of the Revolution* (1955), Premier Nasser of Egypt says that the ceremonials of religious belief should acquire an active economic function. He writes:

> Our view of the Pilgrimage must change. It should not be regarded as only a ticket of admission into Paradise after a long life or as a means of buying forgiveness after a merry one. It should become an institution of great political power and significance. Journalists of the world should hasten to cover the Pilgrimage, not because it is a traditional ritual affording interesting reports for the reading public, but because of its function as a periodic political conference in which the envoys of Islamic states, their leaders of thought, their men learned in every branch of knowledge, their writers, their captains of industry, their merchants and their youth can meet, in order to lay down in this Islamic-world parliament the broad lines of their national policies and their pledges of mutual co-operation from one year to another. Pious and humble, but strong, they should assemble,

stripped of greed, but active; weak before God but mighty against their problems and their enemies; longing for an afterlife, but convinced of their place in the sun, a place they must fill in this existence.[15]

It seems entirely possible therefore, though by no means certain, that the Moslem areas of the world can rebuild a prosperity ethic among their people which will enable them to create prosperity with freedom.

The Islamic world is fortunate in the circumstance that this rebuilding can be done by reviving the economic doctrines of Mohammed in their original purity. The most successful reformations have been based on the idea of restoring the original meanings of old doctrines. The reformation which created the Protestant Ethic was stated by Luther and Calvin in terms of a return to the original intentions of the founders of Christianity. So there is reason to suppose that the theologians of modern Islam can carry out such a transformation in their religion.

IN INDIA. In contrast to its present low position on the scale of prosperity, there was a time when the Indus Valley of India had probably the most prosperous civilization in the world. Between 3000 and 2500 B.C., as excavations at Harappa and Mohenjo-Daro have indicated, there were cities of flourishing trade and culture when there was nothing of that kind in Europe. We know little about the religion of these early centers of relative prosperity, but subsequent peoples who migrated into India from the north seem to have continued their tradition. The *Rig Veda,* a collection of 1028 hymns, dated perhaps 1300 B.C., reveals the great value these people put upon long life, goods, sons, and attempts to control Nature for their own benefit. Unfortunately, about 1000 B.C., this religion suffered a change to an emphasis upon rituals, other-worldliness, and personal meditation, and this anti-prosperity attitude was later crystallized in the doctrines of the Gautama Buddha (563-483 B.C.).[16]

Buddha said that these are the Four Noble Truths of life: (1) suffering exists; (2) its cause is desire; (3) it can be overcome; (4) the right method is the control of wants by psychological and physical exercises.

It is the second of these Truths which concerns the economist directly. It says: "Now this is the Noble Truth as to the origin of suffering. Verily it is the craving thirst that causes the renewal of becomings, that is accompanied by sensual delights,—that is to say, the craving for the gratification of the senses, or the craving for prosperity." [17]

This is in accord with the ancient Hindu philosophy expressed in the Upanishads (800-600 B.C.) which speak of the exhilaration of spirit which comes from being free of demands for earthly things: "A man who is free of desire beholds the majesty of the Self through tranquility of the senses and the mind; and becomes free from grief," says the *Katha Upanishad.* "Such a person is no longer bothered by hunger, thirst, sorrow or confusion. He does not worry about old age and death. He experiences the delight of life and mind, the fullness of peace and eternity." [18]

The logical result of this attitude is described by the Christian theologian Albert Schweitzer, who was one of the thinkers despairing of any material progress in India while these religious views persist. "To Indian thought," he writes, "all effort directed to triumphs in knowledge and power and to the improvement of man's outer life and of society as a whole is mere folly. It teaches that the only sensible line of conduct for a man is to withdraw entirely into himself and to concern himself solely with the deepening of his inner life. He has nothing to do with what may become of human society and mankind." [19]

Miraculous as it may seem, a way has been found to convert these old Hindu and Buddhist attitudes into a stimulation to prosperity. The original kind of Buddhism, called the Hinayana, permitted the individual no concern whatever for other persons or things, but later there arose the Mahayana form of Buddhism which advocated that those about to achieve perfect bliss should consent to postpone their entry into this ultimate Nirvana in order to help others toward it. They were still to have no concern for the prosperity of others, only for their release from wants, yet this proved to be the beginning of a bridge across what had appeared to be the kind of unbridgeable gulf we sometimes see in pictures of the high Himalayan mountains. At least it permitted one want to the wantless, that is, to help others to be wantless; and it permitted action to the actionless, so long as there was no personal gain sought. "To action alone hast thou a right and never at all to its fruits; let not the fruits of action be thy motive," says the *Bhagavad Gita.* "Pitiful are those who seek for the fruits of their action." [20]

But Mahatma Gandhi said of the passage quoted above, "Renunciation of the fruits of action does not mean that there can be no fruits. Fruits are not forbidden. But no action must be undertaken for the sake of its fruits. This is what the *Gita* means." [21]

Thus the way was open for unselfish actions toward others, but still there was no clear statement that these actions should be partly economic in nature until Sarvepalli Radhakrishnan wrote of the Four Ends of Life. These, he said, are (1) to develop our spiritual capacities; (2) to pass through life conscientiously and with knowledge, working out its values and accepting its enjoyments; (3) to sustain and enrich life through material well-being; and (4) to be forbearing and accept such restraints as will harmonize our lives with others.[22]

Concerning the third, or economic end of life, Radhakrishnan writes, "Though it is not its own end, it helps to sustain and enrich life. There was never in India a national ideal of poverty or squalor. Spiritual life finds full scope only in communities of a certain degree of freedom from sordidness. Lives that are strained and starved cannot be religious except in a rudimentary way. Economic insecurity and individual freedom do not go together." [23]

It is impossible to exaggerate the importance for the prosperity of India, and indeed for the whole Orient, of this tremendous philosophical leap into a stimulating interpretation of the ancient religious obligations of Hindus and Buddhists.

However, once we have admitted the economic ends of life to their proper place, there arises the question of the means, and this requires an effort to control Nature. Here a further bar to prosperity arises in Hinduism and Buddhism because of their traditional view dating back to the first century B.C., that Nature as we see it is unreal.[24] There is therefore no point in investigating it, and, according to this view, there is no significant order in it to be discovered by investigation. It is only a play in the sense that sunlight plays on a lake,[25] or a "kind of disagreeable cinema performance which one is compelled to watch, going on in a hall from which one has the greatest difficulty in getting out." One Buddhist patriarch crystallized this view when he said to two monks who were discussing whether a flag was moving by itself, or whether it was being moved by the wind, "Neither the flag nor the wind is moving. There is only a movement within your minds."

Here again, fortunately, Sarvepalli Radhakrishnan has come forward with a reformation of the old doctrine to meet modern needs. On the nature of Nature he says: "Maya does not mean that the empirical world with the selves in it is an illusion, for the whole effort of the cosmos is directed to and sustained by the one supreme self, which, though distinct from everything, is implicated in everything."[26] Yet subsequent statements of Radhakrishnan indicate that he does not quite regard Nature as having equal strength with meditation as a revealer of reality. "For the Hindu thinkers," he writes, "the objective world exists. It is not an illusion. It is real, not in being ultimate, but in being a form, an expression of the ultimate. To regard the world as ultimately real is delusion."[27] And again: "The visible world is the symbol of a more real world. It is the reflection of a spiritual universe which gives to it its life and significance."[28] And yet again: "Human experience is neither ultimately real nor completely illusory. Simply because the world of experience is not the perfect form of reality, it does not follow that it is a delusion without any significance. The world is not a phantom, though it is not real."[29]

These statements seem to be a rather reluctant concession of a degree of importance to Nature, a concession which is likely not to give any great stimulus to Hindus and Buddhists to become scientists, since they would then be spending their lives upon what is thought to be only half-real. We may be reminded of St. Paul's question: "Who shall prepare himself for the battle if the trumpet gives an uncertain sound?"

The sound becomes even more uncertain when we read that according to the doctrine of *maya* as formulated by Sankara, the specially unreal part of Nature is its changes; whereas in Western science, it is precisely the changes, the processes, which seem most interesting and significant to scientists. An understanding of changes seems to be man's best hope of controlling Nature. Yet Sankara tells us that the highest reality is unchangeable and that changing human history has no ultimate reality, although he grants that it is not totally illusory.[30]

There remains to be considered, as a religious obstacle to prosperity in Hindu-Buddhist thinking, the institution of caste. There are innumerable castes, and in each one a person inherits his occupation and cannot change it; he must marry within his caste and he must observe regulations about the acceptance of food and drink from members of other castes. This system developed in the fourth century A.D., and by the fifth century there were also untouchables who had to live apart and give notice of their entrance into town by striking a piece of wood. The presence of a person in a lowly caste is said to be the result of sins he has committed in past lives, and his only hope for promotion to a better caste is in a future reincarnation. In early Hindu times, this promotion depended, so it was decreed, upon certain ritual observances, but later it was emphasized that ethical conduct was more important.

The theory of caste is absolutely incompatible with the prosperity process. That process requires the voluntary movement of each person to his place in one or another of the prosperity groups according to his abilities and interests as ascertained during a thorough education. There is every expectation that in this process sons and daughters will occupy more skilled and more responsible positions than their parents, and there is an inner necessity in the process that the whole spectrum of jobs will move steadily to higher ground as automatic devices take over from the lesser skills. It is of the highest order of importance therefore that the notion of caste be abolished wherever it may still govern the economic destinies of individuals.

Radhakrishnan proposes to abolish caste, even in the minds of the religiously conservative, by pointing out that it was no part of original Hindu or Buddhist doctrine.

Hinduism had been active for fifteen hundred years and Buddhism for a thousand years before the establishment of the caste system which occurred at about the time of the fall of Rome in the West.[31] In the pre-caste period, there had been four classes—priests, chieftains, farmers, and serfs, and Radhakrishnan proposes to retain this fourfold classification in modern life, but to rename the four groups as (1) men of learning and knowledge; (2) men of power and action; (3) skilled craftsmen; and (4) laborers. In the first group there would be the scientists, artists, and philosophers; in the second, the statesmen, politicians, and military leaders; in the third, the leaders of commerce and industry; and in the fourth, those who do the directed work of society.[32]

Radhakrishnan then proposes to build upon this basic classification a Prosperity Ethic very much like some parts of the Protestant Ethic.

> In a real sense, the fourfold scheme is democratic. Firstly it insists on the spiritual equality of all men. It assumes that within every human creature there is a self which has the right to grow in its own way, to find itself, and make its life a full and satisfied image and instrument of its being. Secondly, it makes for individuality in the positive sense. Individuality is attained not through an escape from limitations but through the willing acceptance of obligations. It is erroneous to assume that only the aberrant or the anarchical is the true individual. Thirdly, it points out that all work is socially useful, and from an economic standpoint equally important. Fourthly, social justice is not a scheme of rights but of opportunities. It is wrong to assume that democracy requires all men to be alike. Society is a pattern or an organism in which different organs play different parts. Excellence is specific and cannot be universal. Equality refers to opportunity and not to capacity. While it recognizes that

men are unequal in scale and quality, it insists that every human being shall have the right and the opportunity to contribute to human achievement, as far as his capacity goes. Society must be so organized as to give individuals sufficient scope to exercise their natural energies without being interfered with by others.[33]

It is still uncertain whether the reformation in the religion of India proposed by Gandhi and Radhakrishnan will become dominant. In their pre-reformation condition, Hinduism and Buddhism created an almost perfect recipe for poverty by their emphasis on want-control rather than satisfaction of wants, on the rigidities of caste rather than on economic mobility, and on the unreality of Nature rather than upon its reliability and accessibility to science. The newer interpretations have now joined battle with the old and the outcome will matter a great deal to the one-sixth of the world's population living in India. When we reflect that their numbers are rising by a million persons each month, the need for the victory of their Prosperity Ethic seems very urgent indeed.

IN JAPAN. The Prosperity Ethic in Japan is especially interesting because of its success in a densely populated Oriental nation. This success indicates that there is no inherent natural difference in Eastern and Western ways of thinking which would prevent a meeting of the minds on the subject of prosperity.

There is another point of interest to economists in the fact that the Japanese Prosperity Ethic had in it prior to 1945 two destructive elements—a theory of racial superiority and an ideal of world conquest—both of which had to be purged away before a workable ethic could be achieved.

The idea of the Japanese that they were the chosen race came from the solar theory of Japanese creation which was the central doctrine of the Shinto religion, the official religion of Japan before 1945. According to this belief the islands of Japan were created by two deities who descended from the Sun especially to create this sacred soil. The rest of the land on Earth was made at a later date from mere mud and sea foam.

Finding this new holy land gratifying, the Sun Goddess sent her grandson to rule over it. He, in turn, propagated in direct line the imperial family of Japan whose head, the emperor, was worshipped by the people as an actual living god until 1945. It was in 1868 that Shintoism was made the state religion of Japan and in 1870 the government issued this imperial edict: "We solemnly announce: The Heavenly Deities and the Great Sun Ancestress established the throne and made the succession secure. The line of Emperors in unbroken succession entered into possession thereof and handed it on." [34]

The pro-prosperity side of this solar belief was the immense respect it gave the Japanese for each inch of their Eight Great Islands. The Japanese have become world-famous for their skillful and artistic cultivation of the land with a care that can only be described as worshipful. With their large population in a confined territory it has been indeed a divine blessing to possess such an attitude toward their land, in contrast with the death-dealing waste of resources which characterizes certain other Eastern nations.

An anti-prosperity effect of the solar belief was the idea of Japanese racial superiority which, they said, gave them the right to rule the world, "to bring the whole world under one Japanese roof." The Japanese regarded themselves as collateral descendants of the gods, and under their divine emperor they thought themselves entitled to rule over all lands and peoples. To express disbelief in this view subjected a Japanese citizen to legal prosecution for "dangerous thought." [35]

Following the dialogue of 1940-1945 between Japan and a number of other nations, the Shinto religion was disestablished by the authorities of the Occupation and on January 1, 1946, the emperor issued an edict labelling as false the conception that the emperor is divine and that Japanese people are superior to other races and destined to rule the world. The Imperial Household Ministry ordered that portraits of the imperial family should no longer be kept in sacred repositories in the schools and the Ministry of Education abolished the daily school ceremonies of bowing reverently in the direction of the Imperial Palace and calling out "Long Live the Son of Heaven!" [36]

Looking back upon the twenty years since this surgery upon the economic ethic of Japan, it seems that it has wrought permanent improvement in the economic health of the nation without impairing the basic good the belief had done in creating the distinctive Japanese attitude toward their islands.

Another pro-prosperity part of the Japanese economic ethic has been their willingness to learn about foreign science and technology and to adapt it to their own uses, a trait not characteristic of other Asian nations. It is true that for some 250 years before Commodore Perry sailed into Tokyo Bay in 1853, Japan had deliberately isolated itself from the world, refusing even to allow foreign ships desperately in need of provisions or repairs to enter their ports. But this the Japanese regarded as a necessary precaution to prevent their islands from becoming a Spanish colony.

St. Francis Xavier had arrived in Japan in 1549 and by 1598 there were already three million Japenese converts to Christianity. So the Japanese shut their ports in fear of the fate of other countries in the world where the Spanish flag had landed with Christianity. The only exception to the embargo was the Dutch trading center on an island in Nagasaki Bay, and through this narrow door the Japanese savants, by command of their government, drew the whole Dutch knowledge of science and technology into Japanese hands.[37] Since Commodore Perry's visit, this tendency to adapt Western innovative procedures has been steadily expanded in Japan.

Finally, we might mention as a pro-prosperity factor the multireligious nature of the Japanese family. Japan must surely be unique among nations in encouraging its people to have another religion in addition to Shinto. Provided there was a Shinto altar in the house, there could also be a Christian or a Buddhist shrine. So long as the family accepted the meaning of the sword, the mirror and the necklace handed down by the Sun Goddess, they could also receive the Cross and the Buddha.

Summary

As one essential part of a free economy it is important to attempt to build up in every human being a Prosperity Ethic which will induce him to help himself and others to an economic life of high quality.

The basic model for such an ethic has already been created in the doctrines of Calvin and Luther which we call the Protestant Ethic. There are many who recall this ethic primarily for its emphasis upon work as a vocation rather than a curse, but, in fact, it is much more comprehensive than that. It also contains doctrines of the ethical conduct of business, of the economic duties of the rich, of restraints upon government, of the independence of science, and of the philosophy of consumption. It is practically sufficient as a proper economic stimulus even today. The only needed addition would be a commandment for population control.

This necessary ethic is not coterminous with Protestantism. Some mainly Protestant areas do not have it. Many areas where other religions are predominant do have it, or most of it. We shall have to leave it to another volume to explain its development in other religions and philosophies of life, but the conclusion may be anticipated that in each major view of life there exists a pro-prosperity ethic and an anti-prosperity ethic, and that in various eras and periods one or the other has become dominant. Unfortunately there is no guarantee that a prosperity ethic will not be succeeded by its opposite, as we noted in Islam, nor that the anti-prosperity ethic will not be dominant for many centuries, as in India. If such an ethic is based upon very ancient codes of conduct, it may have destructive elements which need modification, but that this can be done is indicated by the experience of Japan.

What is important for every nation and for every religion and philosophy of life is to see that psychological stimulation of the individual is an essential component of a free economy, and to search out and put together its elements in their own beliefs and their own lives.

Part II

Hurdles on the Path to Prosperity

CHAPTER 7

People versus Resources: the population problem

Whatever religious commandments man may have broken, or bent out of all recognition, one which he has surely observed is to be fruitful and multiply. In one or two hundred thousand years of breeding, he has brought his numbers above three billion souls. And now, with a great leap forward, he expects to double this number in a mere thirty-five years more, that is, to have at least six billion people living on earth in the year 1999.

This prospective increase is so far beyond any firm hopes of increasing the supply of food and other necessities to keep up with it, and there is so little margin above the poverty level for most of the present population, that we are compelled to include population control as a major operating problem of a free economy, at least temporarily.

We say temporarily because the innovative component of capitalism which has given us such surprising gifts as electricity and television, vaccines and aircraft, may yet produce a miracle food to match its miracle drugs, or a new supply of water to make dry land fertile, or adequate space-travel to new worlds, so that there may come a time when it will no longer be desirable to limit the number of humans.

Even now the density of people in the most populous nation, the Netherlands, is about 350 persons per square kilometer as compared with a world average of 25 persons per square kilometer. And the Dutch are a prosperous nation. So if all the world could be brought to the Dutch level of productivity, world population could be fourteen times what it is today without economic disaster. Several geochemists have told us that if the resources of the world were fully utilized it could support as many as 50 billion people.

How Many Humans?

The hard fact now is that it takes two acres of cultivatable land to support a single human being in a kind of Dutch prosperity. From this two acres there come the food and fiber, the lumber and rock and metal, the house-room and factory-room and whatever else is needed to keep this person in reasonable health for three-quarters of a century, to train him to produce more than he consumes and to provide for his comforts, culture, and amusements. At the poverty level of living of the usual underdeveloped nation, one acre per person will do, but it will sustain life only half as long for each person, will not educate him well or keep him healthy, and will seldom comfort, cultivate, or please him.

These rough average figures can give us some understanding of what humanity is up against every day of the year in trying to provide for the 165,000 extra mouths to feed which have appeared in the preceding twenty-four hours. This is not the figure for births, but the excess of births over deaths each day. For every person who dies nowadays, two are born. If the world hopes to support this daily arrival of human freight at the Dutch level, it must find 2 × 165,000 acres of land every day, or somehow squeeze an equivalent increase out of existing land through its innovative procedure. Or, if we are to greet these new arrivals with a poverty level of living, a mere 165,000 new acres per day, or equivalent, will pass muster.

Hope has been raised in some quarters that new worlds in space may provide us with more living room. We could stabilize the population of the earth tomorrow if our space-buses could depart every hour with seven thousand people aboard. From India the schedules would have to be more frequent than from the United States, since the population of India is rising by a million a month, but that of the U. S. by only a million every four months.

The question is whether such transportation could be arranged quickly enough to avert mass starvation among Earth-people. It's a long voyage out, and the passengers would be years, perhaps generations, in transit. And if life on the planets of other stars is as intelligent as life on Earth, our voyagers might meet crowded space-wagons coming the other way—toward us.

But whatever part of the problem cannot be solved in space must be solved on Earth. To stabilize the present population, tens of millions of births a year will have to be prevented. If most of these births occurred in the prosperous countries the problem would be simpler, but in fact, the reverse is true. The poorest nations of the world are increasing their population three times as fast, in percentage terms, as the prosperous nations. And the poorer the nation the greater usually is the rate of increase. According to the United Nations Demographic Yearbook, the annual rate of increase for Mauritania is 5 per cent, for Costa Rica 4 per cent, for Viet Nam 4 per cent, and for the Dominican Republic, 4 per cent, whereas the rate in Europe is 1 per cent. What this means in real numbers can be seen by the forecast for Brazil, which at its present rate of 3.6 per cent can go from 78 million people now to 236 million in 35 years. Human ability in that field is truly astonishing.

The reader should realize that the figures we are using in this section may be 10 to 15 per cent in error one way or the other. The taking of a reliable, regular census is still far from reality in most of the world, and under dictatorships the data gathered are often kept secret. The experience of the past generation has been that expert guesses have consistently underestimated the rate of population growth because methods of death control have spread more rapidly than expected and measures of birth control less rapidly.

In the future this upward trend is likely to be accentuated. Among the 165,000 humans who now die every day, half are under 15 years of age, and two-thirds of these early deaths are preventable by known means. In sum, 50,000 children under 15 die needlessly every day. When medical help begins to arrive in time, that number will be added to the daily increase in the world's population.

Is Numbers Control Natural?

Man's present plight over his expected excess of numbers in relation to his food supply points up a striking difference between himself and the other living creatures who share his planet. Nature seems to have given other forms of life some means of adapting their numbers to the available necessities. And this adaptation mercifully comes into use prior to great need and suffering. There are no bird slums, urban or rural, no tiger or elephant slums, no whale or shark slums or frog slums, no tree slums or lily slums. Has the Creator dealt man a poor hand, denying him both the sure knowledge of how to suport himself on earth, which animals and plants possess instinctively or can learn quickly, and denying him also the apparently automatic control of numbers given to other forms of life?

A potential compensation is the opportunity given to man to work out a method of numbers control for himself, just as he has been given an opportunity to work out a method of making his living which does not bind him to animal routines. The bird, the bear, the beaver, and the bee live now by much the same techniques they used in Homer's time or Nero's, but man does not, or need not. He may choose to develop a better method of living, or he may be passive and fare worse than the animals. Man has now come to a stage in his tenure of the earth at which he must take thought to control his numbers as he has taken thought to improve his products lest the whole human venture come to grief. As this is a new necessity and a reversal of the former need to increase and multiply in order to survive, it is no wonder that so many men and women are disturbed and hesitant about the change.

It may be enlightening at this point to see the forms which numbers control takes in Nature. Ecologists tell us that overbreeding such as we so often see in mankind is not the rule in Nature. As one authority has put it: "Few species ever increase up to the limits of their food supply." [1]

In relation to insects, it has been known for a long time that their high degree of social integration gives them control of their populations. Ants are able to control their total population to prevent pressing upon the food supply and also the numbers in each caste. When there are enough of one type, say soldier ants, reproduction of that group stops. Professor Allee speculates that the mechanism of this control may involve a hormone which is spread around the colony by contact.[2]

Among the birds we find a similar kind of density control through the action of the females. Each species of bird has a characteristic size of clutch, and when the number of eggs in the nest reaches this number the female stops laying eggs. That this is not the most she is capable of may be proven by removing one or more of the eggs. In that case, many kinds of birds will continue to lay eggs until the right number is reached. As Professor Allee remarks, there would seem to be a built-in "psycho-physiological mechanism" that maintains a maximum number of eggs which is presumably the optimum for the species under the given conditions.[3] This mechanism seems to be combined with a sense of territory which leads birds not to overcrowd an area. Even the gentle mourning doves defend their territory while they are building their nests.[4]

When we come to consider animals, we find that territory is a definite consideration. The ancients knew this; they said, "Only one tiger to a hill."

Bodenheimer concludes that:

> The permanent maintenance of large territories per family is therefore a common feature among small and large predators. After this behaviouristic exclusion of food competition, its regulatory function is excluded to a certain degree. The question may be raised—it cannot be answered by the scanty material at our disposal—as to whether the absolute limitation of food itself is at all a common and important limitation in normal environments. Almost all facts available point to the negative.

> It becomes more and more obvious that limitations are primary within the animal itself.[5]

Among rabbits, who are often used as a public symbol of fecundity, the bounty of Nature is used in helpful moderation. Two scientists have come to this conclusion:

> It has been shown that the wild rabbit is a seasonal breeder and in Mediterranean-type climates reproduction is restricted to the period of active growth of pasture plants from autumn to spring. Reproduction ceases before the onset of summer. The timing of reproduction to coincide with the period of greatest food supply, and its cessation before food shortages threaten, automatically safeguards the majority of the young from hunger during their early weeks of growth. Such a mechanism is of high survival value and has undoubtedly been a factor in selection during the evolutionary history of the rabbit.[6]

That Nature can be rapidly flexible in matters of breeding is shown by the short-eared owl whose principal diet is voles. Voles are subject to sharp peaks of population in some years, and in those years the owls increase their egg-laying from the usual five to as many as fourteen and even raise two broods per season. When the population of voles goes down again, the owls return to the usual number of offspring without starvation or overcrowding.

How complicated population behavior can be among animals and, indeed, how little we know about its determinants, has been shown recently by a set of experiments with mice. Although not supposed to be the brightest of God's creatures, mice evidently have ways of their own of limiting their numbers without suffering the Malthusian checks of starvation, pestilence, and war. In the first of three experiments, the mice were confined in large enclosures with a limited food supply; in the second experiment the food was kept limited but the mice were not confined; in the third experiment, they were confined but had unlimited food. In each case, initially, a few couples of wild mice were trapped and established in environments closely resembling their natural habitats, and the researchers kept tab on the changes in their numbers.

In the first experiment, the population grew rapidly to the limit set by the food supply, but not to the point where any mouse lost weight or viability. There was no starvation pressure. Reproduction simply ceased before hunger set in, and did not involve any increase in mortality of old or young. The cessation of reproduction was found to be due to an interruption of breeding by the females, whose reproductive organs became physically involuted. The total population of these mice not only stopped rising, but afterwards declined gradually, providing a margin of safety within the daily limit of food.[7]

In the second experiment, the food supply was kept limited, but the mice were free to leave the colony if they wished to. Usually this type of mouse is very localized in its movements so long as food and cover are available, but it was observed that as the population grew to the point where a daily food shortage was approaching, some of the mice migrated to other locations outside the range of the experiment. The remarkable thing was that this migration took place before any actual food shortage developed.[8]

In the third experiment, six different pens were set up and four pairs of mice established in each one. There was no exit from any pen, but each had plenty of space, plenty of nesting boxes, and an unlimited supply of food. In each pen the population grew, but not indefinitely. At the end of two years all the populations had levelled off. But, although environment appeared to be the same in all the pens, the total population at levelling was quite different.

One pen reached a maximum of 25 mice, another 59, another 81, another 127, another 131, and the last, 138. Each levelling off was accomplished mainly by a sudden drop in the survival of litters. Whereas about nine nestlings in ten had been surviving during the growth period, about nine in ten died at levelling time. But there was no hunger and no evident loss of health among the adults.

There was evidence that Nature was working in this case, also, to restrict births. In two of the pens, the researchers tell us, there was a drop in both birth rates and pregnancy rates. In two others this drop also occurred, but was backed up additionally by a drop in fecundity, as measured by a drop in ovulation among the females and sperm production by the males. In the remaining pens birth rates held up and the levelling of population was accomplished by the mortality of nestlings alone. The researchers suggest that the different population behavior among these pens of mice is to be attributed more to different kinds of social organization than to environmental or physiological factors.[9]

Social organization may go much deeper into Nature than we have been accustomed to think. Even among fish, we are told, at least those in lakes and streams, there are groupings which make it a mistake to imagine these populations as mixtures of isolated individuals swimming at random among one another. On the contrary, fish of a kind seem to swim together in separate watery territories of their own and to govern their numbers to fit with some comfort into their environment.[10]

Even the frogs, basking on their leaves, keep their individual places and distances in the fan-shaped patterns of their groups, though the group may move a hundred yards or more.[11]

The very trees of the forest do not so crowd upon one another that each one lives on the brink of subsistence as so many humans do. On the contrary, trees leave space between them for each one to carry about 50 per cent more leaves than it needs for growth and survival under normal conditions. This excess of foliage may be vital to the tree under unfavorable conditions which may arise from cycles of climate or disease during its lifetime.[12]

Plants, too, have adaptive measures to combat crowding. In corn and other crops, each individual plant produces fewer seeds when the plants are grown closer together than when they are widely spaced. Among the desert annuals in California the seeds will not even bother to sprout in years when there has not been enough rainfall for them to carry through the whole cycle of sprouting, maturing, and bearing new seeds.

Our conclusion is, therefore, that if mankind brings rationality to human breeding it will indicate that man is in that matter acting in the same way that most other living species in Nature act, and not contrary to Nature.

We may even go beyond that and say that by breeding within his means Man will be moving with the trend of Nature, as students of evolution now see it. Professor Allee, a profound and pioneering student of Nature, has summed up this tremendous matter thus:

> Life shows a general progressive change in time. There is an evolution from a less balanced relationship between the internal and external environment to a more closely adjusted relationship. There is also an evolution from limited control of the environment toward much more control of the external environment. These aspects of ecological evolution parallel the evolution of internal physiological balance within the organism.[13]

Rational Breeding

If man reconsiders his place in Nature and takes thought for the morrow in the matter of his numbers, what criteria shall he use to determine whether an additional person should be brought into the world?

One criterion should be whether the prospective child will be able to produce more than he consumes, or at least to earn his keep. The world can not much longer afford to add to its numbers those whose health and training and strength of will are likely to be weak. An old proverb tells us that with every mouth God sends a pair of hands, and, we might add, a brain. And experience tells us that nearly every new human can learn to support himself in one way or another if the proper medical care, education, emotional and physical nourishment, and employment opportunities are made available to him. In considering whether to admit a new member to the human club at a particular time, therefore, its prospective parents need to consider whether they and their community together are likely to provide these means to a productive life.

Another consideration is the effect a new member will have on the family. Will he overstrain the budget and force one or both parents to take on excessively fatiguing work to earn money—or perhaps to ask for public charity? Will bearing him and raising him harm the mother physically? Will he overstrain the parents emotionally? Every parent has a limit of nervous capacity in dealing with children, and there comes a point where one more child will cause emotional impoverishment or a hostile atmosphere for the whole family. Will the newcomer extend the child-rearing years of the parents beyond a reasonable time? After bearing a few children, many women fear another one whose raising and education will deprive them of well-earned years of freedom and personal activity. The prospective father may take into account the probable elimination of long-cherished hobbies or travels or business ventures if he is called upon to finance another child all the way through higher education. We no longer think it fair that the whole adult life of parents should be devoted to their children.

In the present state of things, humanity has a right to expect every couple to undertake conscientious thought and full discussion and conscious decision before inviting a new life into the world.

The Causes of Irrational Breeding

The advantages of rational breeding are so great that we may wonder why any couple has too many children. Some years ago it was popular to think that if parents only had more information about preventing unplanned births the problem would be solved. Now we realize that there are strong economic, emotional, and theological pressures on the side of overbreeding.

It may seem strange to say that any economic pressures favor overlarge families, but there are certain common distortions of the economic environment of a family that may produce this result. Most families in the world still live on the land and scrape it with poor tools to earn a meager living. They act upon the idea that the more children they have the more help there will be with the endless chores. Also the parents are made constantly aware of the grim fate which awaits an older couple if there are not enough children to support them—and most people grow old and ill in their forties in the world as it is today.

Such couples know that some of the children will not survive, but to them this only means they must bear more to achieve their purposes. In many parts of the world also, daughters are not considered valuable, and so the parents breed even more excessively to achieve a certain number of sons.

Another type of pressure towards overbreeding is the emotional need that children fill in the lives of some poor people. In many countries, a man's idea of his own manhood is dependent upon his keeping his wife pregnant, and often another woman, too. For other couples, a feeling of guilt about failure in life is assuaged by having extra children. A large family may also give a sense of identity to parents lost in a mass proletariat.

There are also theological pressures to be considered. In the poor nations, some religious leaders find an argument for unrestricted breeding in the concept of the value of suffering. This world, they say, is only a proving ground for eternity, and one proof that the individual can give of his fitness for heaven is his ability to suffer with resignation. Under this view, it is cruel to deny a child his little span on earth, no matter how painful.

Finally, let us mention another group of causes of overbreeding which may be lumped together under the term "passivity complex." It is astonishing how many people in the world believe in a fixed destiny. What will be will be. A belief in fixed destiny, when it leads to lack of foresight in breeding, or is simply an excuse for a lack of foresight, helps create large families for whom there is little prospect of lives of satisfying quality.

Overbreeding, therefore, may not be simple to overcome. It may be stubbornly rooted in a number of circumstances, pressures, beliefs, and psychological habits.

A Good Hope

Each achievement in making population changes more rational helps to increase the prosperity of human beings.

And by a stroke of good fortune, increases in prosperity tend to rationalize still further the changes people desire to make in population. This means that once humanity begins to accept responsibility for the numbers problem it can expect help from the process itself. The mutual interaction of population and prosperity is so important and so hopeful that it may be worthwhile to consider what factors in prosperity lead to more rational decisions about population.

1. As new ideas favorable to material progress spread through a community there arise new family ambitions towards a steadily higher standard of living. A better home, financial security, an opportunity to develop talents and abilities, higher education for the children—such things become more important psychologically than having numerous offspring if that means remaining poor.

2. Another factor reinforcing numbers control as prosperity rises is the necessity of more and more years of higher education, reaching into the late teens for most people, the early twenties for many, and late twenties for those who hope for the highest accomplishments. Without this extended training the employed person in modern prosperous society has little hope of satisfying the new family ambitions; and the more years he can spend in advanced training the higher his lifetime income is likely to be. The upshot is that marriage is commonly postponed, in prosperous countries, from the teens to the twenties, thus by-passing the most fertile and overconfident years.

3. The rising ambition of the family in prosperous societies is closely related to a new higher status for women, and this acts to lower the birth rate. As women achieve political and professional status, and as higher education becomes general among them, their ideal becomes the

family of two or three children who can be raised, educated, and seen into homes of their own, still leaving the mother many years of free and interesting life. The educated woman acquires other ideals in life than unceasing service to "children, church, and kitchen."

4. Another factor influencing population which is closely entangled with the others we have mentioned is the degree of urbanization and suburbanization that come with prosperity. The typically poor nation of our day has about 80 per cent of its people on the land, living on lonely farms or in rural villages of a few hundred people each. In a prosperous nation more than two-thirds live in towns or cities or the suburbs of cities, leaving less than a third to raise the food and fiber for the rest. Historically, such urbanization has always meant a loss of fertility; it is probably a tenable generalization to say that great cities such as Rome, Athens, Alexandria, Paris, and London have never maintained their populations by reproduction, but have depended for keeping up their numbers upon a continual influx of youngsters from the farms.

Man may therefore take encouragement in going forward with increases in prosperity and with rationality in changing his numbers, secure in the high probability that advances in either area will encourage favorable changes in the other.

A possible view to the contrary needs to be dealt with. Forecasts of increasing population in developed nations are often hailed as good omens of brisk business, since the newcomers will need to be provided with all the gear regarded as essential to the good life. Would a stabilized population lose this stimulus to prosperity? The answer is, not necessarily. There is an old saying that money doesn't care who spends it, and if an equivalent amount of money is laid out for improving the quality of life for those already living, the economy will not suffer a loss of stimulation. Of course, if the money which would have been spent is left idle and if this results in idle productive powers in the economy, then some depressive effect would occur.

Conclusion

We might, with a character of Shakespeare's, say:

> All the world's a stage,
> And all the men and women merely players:
> They have their exits and their entrances;
> And one man in his time plays many parts.

Yet it is a peculiar stage. More than 300,000 new actors make their entrances each day, and only about half that number make their exits. Almost any pair of male and female performers can, by playing their respective parts, bring a new actor onto the stage. And, contrary to theatrical practice, the new actors do not know in advance what part they will play. Being very young at their first appearance, they will have to be trained on the stage itself, perhaps for a mean part beneath their talents, perhaps for a regal role whose costumes will hang in lapping folds around them. As the cast grows larger the stage may become so crowded that no one has room to make his proper entrance, to strut a noble part, or be carried off in a dignified position when his last scene is done.

Fortunately, some of the actors helpfully spend their time building additions to the stage while the play goes on. Others demonstrate their truculence by tearing parts of it down, and whether more will be built than torn down is not known, since the play is a mystery-drama whose ending is not agreed upon by the actors, though some claim to know the intentions of the Author.

Now on this crowded stage a new rehearsal is beginning in which couples may learn to play the part of man and wife without adding to the cast more actors for whom there will be only meager parts. By thus limiting the cast, there will be resources available for making the stage larger, providing better backgrounds and wardrobes, improving the direction, and giving more of the actors roles of satisfying quality.

CHAPTER 8

Taking the Good and Avoiding the Bad: the automation problem

Automation is one of the most recent results of the innovative component of our economy. In some ways it is new, in that some mental processes which were formerly carried out by the human brain can now be done by machinery. And when the physical-process machines are coupled with the new brain-process machines, quite spectacular production can be achieved with very little direct labor.

Automation may also be viewed as the latest in a long line of steps toward prosperity. As the economist sees human history, man appeared first as a forager for food among the plants and animals he found about him. Later he settled down to cultivate both plants and animals and supplemented his comforts with a few handicrafts—a bit of pottery here, a little weaving there, and brewing. Then he discovered that by using tools upon the soil some of the people could raise food for all of the people, and those released from toil in the fields could spend their time on the handicrafts. Still later, by applying tools, including machines, to making the handicrafts, some workers could be released from work upon these so-called secondary products (food and fiber being primary) to work at the tertiary level—the personal services, the clerical work, and the professional vocations.

And we may look forward to a time when the professions predominate, when the dark-coat jobs of bankers, lawyers, executives, and teachers and the white-coat jobs of doctors, scientists, and technicians will be more numerous than the traditional blue-collar and white-collar jobs. This is the transformation that automation can accomplish—the shift to a predominantly professional society.

It is remarkable that economists have never pinned a name on this progressive shifting of predominant human occupations from the forest to the plain to the farm, to the factory, to the office, to the professional suite, as a nation climbs the ladder to prosperity. Since it has the appearance of a shifting motion, perhaps it could be called the "shiftover," or, with the hope that it might be a smooth transition, the "slideover." At a local conference recently an industrial executive suggested that a good name for it might be the "pullover," indicating that new occupations pull people away from old ones. But a union executive who had had some trouble with displacement of his constituents by machinery preferred the term "pushover."

There is a fear that automation may spread so quickly through factories and offices, laboratories, and classrooms that people will have no time to prepare for it, and "full unemployment" will ensue. Although the future is notoriously unpredictable, this fear of instant automation seems to be unfounded. It seems more probable that automation, like other industrial revolutions before it, will be adopted in a Schumpeterian manner, first surging forward, then slowing down, coming in strongly in part of the economy at one surge, then after a lull, perhaps of some years, advancing into another part of the economy during the next surge.

Fear of sudden automation throughout the economy arises usually from too narrow a consideration of the factors governing investment in automated processes. If one takes the prevailing descriptions of possible automatic systems on a purely technical basis, there would seem to be no reason to hesitate in installing them at once, displacing practically everybody. But in society as it really is, investment is not technocratic, that is, ruled solely by technical possibilities, but econocratic—ruled by considerations of cost and profit, of the efficiency and flexibility of comparable processes, of the dangers of rigidity, future competition, and similar considerations.

We might remember that the political movement called Technocracy told us several decades ago that a single plant operated by several men could turn out all the bricks needed in the United States. Yet such a plant has never been built. No one has appeared who is willing to put up the great sum of money which would have to be risked against the possibility that some other building material might displace bricks, or that costs of shipping bricks from the central factory might price them out of local markets in competition with local plants, or that a newer method of making bricks might make the whole great automated plant suddenly obsolete. Instead, we find in brickmaking today a combination of improving automatic processes—ovens, conveyer belts, and packaging machines interspersed on the assembly line with a great deal of human labor which loads, inspects, watches, turns knobs, moves levers, drives vehicles, and adjusts and repairs the machines and the measuring devices.

We may feel sure that the human being is far from obsolete in our economy. It is still true, as one engineer put it, that a human being is the only 180-lb. servo-mechanism that can be mass-produced by unskilled labor. It is also true that the human being is by far the most flexible of all cybernetic machines, because he has the ability to turn his attention with astonishing ease from one task or process to another without being rebuilt each time. It was this fact which led the Ford Motor Company to abandon an automated engine factory after it found that in order to change the design of the engine to keep up with competition almost the entire factory had to be rebuilt. This incident shows clearly the difference between technical possibilities and wise economic choices. A technological world might for a time create massive displacements, but we live in an econological world which makes its advances more slowly.

There would seem to be no reason therefore to expect a sudden wave of automation to overwhelm the ability of mankind to make the necessary adjustments.

But there is also no ground for a shallow optimism that the essential adjustments will always be automatic. Some economists of truly classical optimism have tried to prove that technical changes always create more demand for labor than they displace. What they actually have shown so far is only that there are conditions under which this can occur, but it is not inevitable. If the new processes require large investments, their manufacture may create more jobs even before any displacement occurs, and the number of new jobs may exceed the number displaced for a long time. And if the displaced persons can easily find new jobs suited to their abilities the social trouble will be minimized. It is always most helpful to this adjustment if the economy is in an expansionary phase, with new kinds of goods and services coming into view and with a good deal of enthusiasm for them among producers and consumers. These conditions were met, for example, when the automobile displaced the horse and buggy.

It is clear that such favorable conditions are not always to be expected and that from time to time special arrangements will have to be made to assist personal adjustments to automation.

The Choices Automation Offers

What automation does offer to the United States and to other developed nations is a release of productive energies—land, labor, capital, and management—just as other industrial revolutions have done. At what rate this productive power will become available is not yet clear, but we may note that the present rise in output per man-hour in the United States is approaching the magnitude observed during the 1920's when the assembly-line method of production was the industrial revolution of the day.

It seems safe to predict that the release of productive power will be substantial and there are three ways in which it can be used, depending upon the choices the developed economies make.

1. It can be used to create concentrated areas of leisure. Whole groups can be freed from work. Economists Michael Harrington and Robert Theobald have proposed granting a guaranteed annual income to every family in the United States. The amount might be about $4000 per year for a family and about $2500 per year for a single person, and this would change with the cost of living and the standards of society and also with the political power of the recipients.

It seems likely that large numbers of the present low-income groups would withdraw from work altogether under such an arrangement. If the head of a family was earning $3000 per year, his guaranteed income allotment would be the extra $1000 required to make up the minimum. If he earned $4001 per year, he would get nothing from the guaranteed income fund. In effect, he would be working as a dollar-a-year man.

2. Another choice would be to use the liberated energy under a full-employment program to meet the world's needs. The planet Earth is still a long way from being a fully comfortable place for human life. In the developed nations there is a galaxy of situations called "urban problems," including crime, pollution, ugliness, crowding, and tension. All of them could be substantially relieved by applying productive powers. And the underdeveloped nations are facing a period of actual mass starvation as their expanding populations outrun their weak ability to produce even the necessities of life. In those countries, taken as a group, the man-food ratio started to fall five years ago and the number of children growing up illiterate and without productive skills is increasing. Even managerial competence is decreasing in many underdeveloped economies as foreign executives are expelled and as the few young local executives are increasingly taken into the service of their military establishments.

3. The third choice is a system of distributed leisure. This would set a goal of full employment for the economy but would see to it that each person's working life would be punctuated by more periods of leisure. This could take many forms. More holidays, longer week-ends, sabbatical years, shorter work weeks, shorter work days, month-long vacations in both summer and winter. As far as possible

each working person could be given a choice of the pattern of his distributed leisure.

It may be useful to indicate some of the pros and cons of these three broad choices.

The great advantage of concentrated leisure is that it would remove at once the difficult problems of finding jobs for low-income people. They are the hardest to place and they require the most personal reconstruction to make them acceptable to employers. There is a great deal of doubt whether some of them can ever meet the rising qualifications for even the basic jobs which are one feature of the advance of automation. Guaranteed incomes would provide a simple replacement for the wide variety of social services and charity favors by which these people now accumulate an income piece by piece.

The large risk of concentrated leisure is that we are not at all sure of the political and social behavior of masses of people who have nothing to do. The Roman Empire found that its unemployed men would not rest content with bread and circuses. Instead they formed an internal proletariat and, when the barbarians breached the frontiers, the proletariat helped tear down the Empire, stone by stone. In modern times, the city of Los Angeles has found itself partly destroyed by mobs of people of working age who were not grateful for relief payments, television, and a champion baseball team. Chronic alienation and sporadic revolt may be a characteristic of mass leisure.

In fact, mass leisure could become the equivalent of Marx's reserve army of the unemployed which he hoped would be a major tool in overthrowing capitalism.

There is a problem here in the psychology of receiving. Religious leaders tell us that it is better to give than to receive. It may be easier as well. The psychology of giving is known. It is beneficial within the limits of Yeats's warning that "too much sacrifice makes a stone of the heart." But when a person receives all his income from another without being required to give anything in return, he may turn hostile to the giver, and, far from being grateful, may wish to injure the benefactor even though the recipient's income would be lessened. When a person receives everything, he may become angry because he hasn't achieved the level of income and self-respect that the giver possesses. Part of the puzzle is that this isn't always true. Some children love their parents even though the parents provide everything without strings. And, at the social level, we see that thousands of families in Appalachia have lived peaceably on relief for three generations.

There has been very little human experience with mass leisure among low-income groups, but there has been a great deal more with leisure among the rich. Throughout most of history, the commonest arrangement has been to leave the upper-income group free from work, and the results were not encouraging. Some aristocrats devoted their time to the arts of peace, but the arts of war, conquest, destruction, and slavery were never neglected. So when we fear that the leisured poor might not be able to amuse themselves peacefully, we are not really making a distinction between them and the rich.

An important problem of the second alternative, a full-employment policy, would be to raise the skill and reliability of many of the present low-income people who have never had jobs of the kind that automated production requires.

The skills required are not so extraordinary; they consist of solid ability in reading, writing, and arithmetic, so that the employee may be able to read instructions accurately and follow them, report results and problems to his superiors in clear language, and make elementary computations on the job with speed and sureness. Unfortunately, our schools do not make all of their pupils competent in these matters.

The demand for reliability is increased as automation spreads. Automatic machines are fast and expensive, and breakdowns and mistakes are far more costly than with earlier techniques. So the human operator must be on the job, he must watch the right dials, push the right buttons, sound the right alarms, and take the right action to head off costly damage. Older techniques allowed a great deal more leeway.

If the developed nations use their full-employment policy together with automation to produce more goods to help the poorer nations through the impending crisis of overpopulation, then there would be problems to be solved in the technique of foreign aid. It would have to be much larger than now, at least ten times as large, until the "population hump" had been gotten over, and politicians would have to reassess the experience of the preliminary period of foreign aid from 1946 to the present to be sure that the new foreign aid would be effective. Especially there would need to be requirements that the poorer nations be making genuine progress on their own in constructing the components of capitalism and in meeting the problems of population and inflation as a condition of aid. Continuation of indiscriminate, unsupervised, and unconditional aid would be an act of folly in the coming struggle against starvation and dictatorship among most of the human race.

The third alternative—distributed leisure—is attractive as a way of using the extra energy automation will make available partly because it would involve only an extension of the periods of leisure we already have. The techniques are known and the dangers are minimal. Evidently we are going to need additional leisure, anyway, in order to keep life interesting for those who tend automatic machines. There is little doubt that such jobs will be less interesting and absorbing and lonelier than non-automated jobs, and yet at the same time the nervous strain may be greater because of the continuous alertness and great responsibility. We have had evidence of this already in the fatigue of airline pilots sitting and watching their dials while automatic devices fly the planes. There will need to be more leisure for active and constructive hobbies and human relationships to keep life interesting as automation progresses.

The disadvantages of distributed leisure are two. First it creates the same problem as a full-employment policy—the need to build into almost everybody in the low-income groups a higher level of skill and reliability to make them worth hiring. Second, it may bring feelings of guilt about the extra goods for the world's needs that might have been produced during the extended periods of leisure. How uncomfortable these feelings may be will depend upon how intensely the people of the developed nations come to feel responsible for the fate of all humanity.

The three alternatives we have been discussing can be mixed to some degree, but it would seem wise for the developed nations to make some conscious choice of one of them as their predominant response to automation, with adequate provision for reconsideration from time to time.

Dangers of Cyberculture

Looking into the far future is not a science, but it may be interesting to imagine a time when population control has been achieved, when synthetic food to nourish life comes plentifully from factories, when fresh water is cheap in every desert place, and when automated processes can supply everyone everywhere with the requirements for a long, healthy life. What will man do then?

Some social philosophers believe that life in that time, if it ever comes, will be so different from any we have known that it will deserve a new name, and they suggest calling it "cyberculture."

Some gloomy predictions have been made about the age of cyberculture, especially by the eminent scientist, Professor Norbert Wiener of the Massachusetts Institute of Technology. Professor Wiener was an inventor of the mathematics which made automation possible, and he confesses feelings of guilt about what he may have loosed upon humanity similar to the feelings Einstein expressed about his contribution to the atomic bomb.

In his books *The Human Use of Human Beings* (1950) and *God and Golem, Inc.* (1964), Dr. Wiener anticipates four disasters from automation.

1. Full unemployment when all factories are automated and idle while the population starves in the streets for lack of purchasing power to buy what the factories could produce.
2. The devaluation of the human mind by machines that can outwit man in games of skill and in control of machinery.
3. The shock to human pride when man discovers that there are machines that can reproduce themselves. Dr. Wiener expects this to be as emotionally upsetting to man as was Darwin's theory of evolution.
4. The possible destruction of mankind by decision-making machines that fail to take into account man's desire for survival.

Dr. Wiener's fear that full unemployment must lead to an absence of purchasing power is not realistic in view of modern economic techniques. Supposing that things ever do get as cornucopic as Wiener pictured them, it would simply be necessary to supply people with money to make it profitable for the button-owners to put their fingers to the buttons. To supply purchasing power would require no invention of marvellous new devices, but simply an extension of present monetary procedures. We often supply income to people for other reasons than as a reward for producing things. We give a great deal of money to children, veterans of wars, and the unemployed to enable them to live while they are being educated or re-educated. We give money to the old and sick who will never produce again. We give money to needy families. Thus the concept of minimum incomes, apart from work, for the purpose of keeping families in the human race is already in operation for some, and its scope would need only to be extended to prevent Dr. Wiener's first disaster if that should ever threaten.

Even in a fully automated world, the extra purchasing power would need to be only a supplement. A substantial amount of income would be distributed by the automated firms in repairing, replacing, and innovating their equipment. And even though there would be little income from direct labor, people would still receive rents, interest, and dividends in return for the use of their property and their funds. The circulation of income by government—money raised by taxes and by borrowing—might have to be somewhat larger than now, but if the automated world were also a warless world, a distribution of money for military production might be replaced by its distribution for social purposes. Provision of adequate purchasing power for an automated world could therefore be economically smooth.

As for Dr. Wiener's second disaster, it is true that a machine was able to beat a scientist who was not a good checker player, and it is also true that, when thus stimulated to learn how to play better, the scientist beat the machine. The machine was then so programmed that it could review its moves and decide not to repeat those which led to defeat, and there ensued a learning race between man and machine.

Is it frightening that man can be defeated in a game of wits by a machine he has created? It is not frightening economically, since men do not in the ordinary course of business invest in machines in order to engage in contests with them. The relationship which justifies the expenditure of money to make or buy the machine is one of co-operation, of using human strength and brains in the same direction as machine strength and brains to improve productivity. A businessman does not buy a truck in order to engage it in a game of tug-of-war, which he would lose, nor does he spend a large sum of money on a computer for the purpose of engaging in a memory contest against its information-storage unit. He would lose that contest, too, just as he would lose a contest in long division with his calculating machine. The important thing is that the human can select the type of relationship he has with machines, and economic logic dictates a co-operative one.

As for his third disaster, Professor Wiener assures us that machines are on the way which can create a package containing necessary directions and materials for creating another machine. He uses the analogy of the hen and the egg, and foresees the development of machine genetics. Shall we be alarmed over the prospect that some machines of the future will be self-reproductive?

We think not. Throughout most of his history man has used bio-tools, that is, instruments which had the ability to multiply themselves. He has had his cattle, his chickens, and his hogs. He has used these animals as bio-factories to convert grains and grasses into the proteins of meat. The grain was self-reproductive, and so were the bacteria that helped make cheese and wine, and the horses and oxen that brought these things to barn and cellar. Bio-machines are an old story to mankind.

It will be a different matter, of course, if the reproductive abilities of some machines get out of hand and start flooding the landscape with, say, calculators or translators or wallpaper machines. There will have to be a club handy to knock the prolific parent on the transducer and put a stop to it. If matters have gone too far, perhaps machinicides will have to be sprayed on, or destructive electric currents. Foresight may lead to the incorporation in certain machines of sterilization circuits which can be activated if things get too rabbity. Fortunately, most machines can be isolated if they run wild. A machine reproducing itself would have to be fed materials and currents to continue this process, and these supplies could be cut off. Even a chicken has to eat to continue laying eggs.

We might remember that man has had a long experience with at least one tool that is fiercely self-reproductive—fire. And he has been able to use and control it within tolerable limits, although some of the newer forms of atomic fire are still difficult to control.

Most of all, Dr. Wiener fears the fourth disaster he mentions, the malfunction of decision-making machines, especially the machine that might be developed to decide when a nation should launch an atomic war. Such a machine, Dr. Wiener says, would have to be carefully programmed not to achieve victory alone, but to include survival and other desirable goals in reaching its decisions. Machines making lesser decisions must also be carefully programmed and carefully watched, he says, to make sure that their goals are our goals.

One possibility is that all machines making decisions of consequence should be accompanied by a human arbiter to monitor their results and prevent the wilder actions which might otherwise result. In the launching of missiles, human arbiters are already used to see that a missile which veers dangerously off-course is destroyed in mid-flight. As this principle is applied, a new group of highly responsible jobs will be created.

The Personality of Cyberman

A vast gulf lies between the personality of the first primitive human hunter and that of the present-day scientist, teacher, machinist, or industrialist. When we look back over human history it is astonishing to see how malleable mankind has been. Other forms of life on Earth—the bird, the beaver, and the bear—stay much the same from age to age, but man has changed as his work has changed, and each change has provoked fears.

As hunters became farmers, there was fear that their virtues of individualism, self-reliance, and personal courage would be lost, and popular drama still presents the images of Daniel Boone, the American Indian, and the hard-riding horsemen of the Eurasian steppes as noble archetypes. When farmers moved to urban work, again there was fear, this time of the effects of the crowded squalor in the slums around the "dark, Satanic mills." And when the children of factory workers grew up and took white-collar jobs there was concern among social commentators over their loss of muscular power, their pallid countenances, and the deadening of human spontaneity by what Charles Lamb called "the sad, dull drudgery of the desk's dry wood."

What further changes in human personality may we expect in a fully automated society?

For one thing there will be less emphasis on work as a duty and more emphasis on work as a self-chosen purpose in life. The idea of work has changed its nature more than once in human experience. Work was once the product of force—something the man on horseback imposed upon the man on foot. Then it became, in medieval Europe, the means of working off a curse incurred by Adam and Eve. After the Protestant Reformation, work became a duty which gave life meaning and sanctity, especially if done conscientiously with a view toward service to others.

In an automated society, there would be much less need of work to help others. Such an economy would provide the needs of life for everyone with little human labor. Most human beings would then be in position to choose a mission or a succession of missions in life on some other basis than the economic needs of themselves or of humanity.

Actually such a choice would correspond with the kind of work first mentioned in the Bible. In Genesis we find it said that before the creation of Eve "the Lord God took the man and put him into the garden of Eden to dress it and keep it." And then, Genesis says, God made all the birds and beasts and brought them to Adam to be named. It would be these original, decorative, and scientific kinds of work which could be expected to increase for cyberman.

We might also expect less emphasis upon what man builds in the world and more emphasis upon what he builds within himself. Keynes was an advocate of this change. He tells us that his personal religion was derived from the doctrines of Professor G. E. Moore, the Cambridge philosopher who taught that the highest morality consisted in living a life of successive "beautiful states of mind." These were to be accumulated by seeking experiences in relation to nature, art, literature, friendship, and love. Keynes suggested that there might be some order, structure, or mode of progression in each person's collection, but he did not press the point. He and his friends in the Bloomsbury Group—Leonard Woolf and his wife, Virginia, the novelist, Roger Fry, the painter, Lytton Strachey, the essayist, and the others—sought one beautiful experience after another as their goal in life. Although some of them had to work now and again to support themselves, or to fulfill what they felt to be public duties, they did not attribute any high moral value to work.[1]

There would surely be great gains in the range and quality of human experience if the kind of life Keynes advocated should become available to ordinary human beings. But there would also be losses, just as there were when the primitive hunters first settled down to farming. In cyberman, the principal loss might be the feeling that his existence was important to others and to the world and even to God's plans, a feeling satisfied by hard work for serious purposes. In cyberculture it would be harder for anyone to feel indispensable. Human beings would need to develop a philosophy of the value of existence based upon other experiences than work.

It is tempting to go on with further exploration of the personality of cyberman, but his problems are not really as urgent as some social commentators would have us believe. When we look at the economic condition of the world as it is and reflect how far we are from supplying plentifully to everyone the ten kinds of goods and services we have defined as "prosperity," we can see that for at least one century and probably for more than one, work will be the only means to a decent human condition.

CHAPTER 9

Choosing Between the All-Go and the Go-Stop Economy: the inflation problem

The adoption of an anti-depression procedure as one component of capitalism, in response to the Keynesian Amendment to the theory of capitalism, has eliminated deep depressions. And they will remain eliminated as long as the politicians in power are willing to use the procedure. It is encouraging that there has not been a major depression in any nation that has set up such a procedure, whereas, prior to Keynes it was normal to expect one serious depression in nearly every decade and an almost catastrophic one at least once in nearly every generation. Thus a very great advance has been made in the conduct of economic affairs among free men. The percentage of unemployment in the industrial nations used to swing between zero and forty-five; now it swings between zero and about 7 or 8 per cent. And this improvement has been made in one generation!

The Go-Stop Economy

One might think that economists would be satisfied with so great an accomplishment, but some are not. They want to eliminate even the present relatively gentle swings of unemployment. What we have now, they say, is a go-stop economy. To illustrate this, suppose that we are starting at the point in the cycle when the economy is in a recession (the common name for a mild depression), with unemployment, at, say, 7 per cent. Then stimulative measures are applied. These include more government spending, lower taxes, special tax favors for new private investment, lower interest rates, easy lending terms in the money market—the whole anti-depression program. Political flags are run up bearing the message, "Let's get the country going again."

So the country does get going again. Industry and trade become more active. Employment is up, wages are up, profits are up, the stock market is up. Incumbent politicians are easily re-elected. Optimism is rife.

But, as part of this same package of prosperity, prices also rise and the nation's purchases and gifts abroad increase. These are regarded as danger signals. Flags labelled "Inflation!" and "Adverse Foreign Balance!" are run up; all the motors of the anti-depression procedure are thrown into reverse; and a recession is produced which almost stabilizes prices and almost eliminates the adverse foreign balance while increasing unemployment.

Before the danger signals can be reduced to zero, however, a cry against so much unemployment goes up, politicians not in office see their chance, and the whole campaign to get the country going again starts afresh. We have come full cycle. And we have been through several such cycles in many of the developed nations in the last twenty years.

The All-Go Economy

There are economists who want to see the free nations rise to a higher level than go-stop provides and have full employment all the time. They want to remove the injustices of unemployment; they want to make available the extra 4 or 5 per cent per year in the value of the Gross National Product that full employment would provide. In the United States, as of 1966, that would mean about thirty billion dollars' worth of goods and services annually. That is about ten times the present level of foreign aid. Think, these economists say, how much aid that much product could give in the way of needed personal income, needed public services, needed capital improvement in industry, needed financing of art, literature, science, recreation, and every other cultural activity. It would be enough to finance a new Renaissance!

The Costs of an All-Go Economy

A completely "go" economy, with nearly full employment all the time, would be a step forward in the co-evolution of freedom and prosperity. And it could be achieved by operating the anti-depression procedure most of the time instead of only some of the time. The question is, what would be the costs?

LOSS OF PRICE STABILITY. One of the costs would be the abandonment of the cherished ideal of price stability. Under an "all-go" economy, the cost of living could be expected to rise by at least 2 per cent per year and perhaps by as much as 5 per cent per year. Why is this true?

The principal reason is that when employment is full, consumers have rising incomes and spend confidently, increasing their borrowings to do so. And businessmen, seeing their inventories shipped off to customers as fast as they come in, find it possible and profitable to raise their prices without losing much, or any, volume of business.

Some economists have proposed that to eliminate price increases, an all-go economy could be coupled with a nationwide system of price controls. Such a program, however, would be most unwise. It would be impossible to enforce price control without damaging the basic freedoms of a free economy. Even in wartime, national price controls were difficult to administer, though necessary. In peacetime, they would be impossible unless controls were extended to quantity and quality as well as price. Nearly every businessman, when price controls are put upon his products, can evade them by reducing the amounts he provides the customers—fewer ounces in the can, less sugar in the candy, fewer threads in the garment, fewer parts in the television set, and so on endlessly.

If the government, in response to these evasions, puts an army of inspectors to watching the quantities, then the businessman can evade by changing the quality of his products—putting less costly elements in the paint, poorer ores in the steel, hastier workmanship in the suit and all that. By the time another army of inspectors has regulated the quality of every product and service, freedom would have vanished.

It is also true that if prices in general are regulated, wages must be controlled. This opens a new box of troubles, since employees can evade the intent of the regulations by lowering the quantity and quality of the work they supply in return for wages which they consider unsatisfactory. It would be necessary to employ another army of standard setters and observers to police these evasions, and in the end there would be another loss of energy and freedom in the economy.

Under present conditions of countervailing power, the regulation of wages would also call forth demands for regulating profits, interests, and rents, and such regulations would serve to diminish still further the initiative and energy upon which a free economy depends to keep itself prosperous.

Another reason for avoiding price control in an all-go economy is that much of the stimulation to spend and invest which makes for full employment in such an economy arises from the expectation that prices will continue to creep up in future years. When businessmen expect the costs and returns on buildings to keep going up, they are in a hurry to invest in new buildings now rather than later. And when a new steel plant built now, or an apartment house built now, can count upon rising returns to its owners over a period of years, then there is a built-in extra anticipation of profits which warrants a larger investment than would seem profitable if prices were expected to be stable over the years. The prospect of mild inflation is highly stimulating to private investment.

The same is true for consumer spending. If prices for houses, cars, and appliances are expected to go a little higher year by year, the consumer is inclined to buy now rather than later. This circulates money faster than it would circulate under conditions of stable prices and helps the economy to remain at full employment.

Ratio Thinking. In an all-go economy, therefore, the consumer would have to revise his attitude towards a steady climb in the cost of living. At present, whenever an increase is announced from one month to another, there is much shaking of heads and reminiscence about lower prices in the good old days, while newspapers editorialize sadly or angrily over the shrinking value of the dollar as a sign of the decay of the nation. In an all-go economy, the consumer would have to measure his gain by comparing the rise in his income after taxes with the rise in the cost of living. If, in a given year, his income had gone up by 6 per cent and the cost of living by 3 per cent, he would have to count himself better off. Even though the value of each dollar he earns would have diminished by 3 per cent in that year, he would have to console himself with the thought that the increase in the number of dollars coming in to him had more than made up the difference.

Some attempt at ratio thinking is necessary to reconcile the consumer to the degree of inflation which has taken place in the developed countries even within living memory. In the United States since 1900, for example, the cost of living has tripled. This is in itself a sad figure unless it is coupled with the fact that personal income per capita after taxes has risen by nine times in the same period. To give another example, in the fifteen years between 1947 and 1962, the cost of living in the United States rose by 37 per cent, but this was more than offset by a rise of personal income per capita after taxes by 74 per cent in the same period.

Another sacrifice in public thinking which would be called for by an all-go economy would be the end of hope for a return to the good old days of lower prices. Gratifying reductions in the prices of newly-developed goods could be expected, but the general level of prices would never return to what it was in grandmother's day. In an all-go economy, the emphasis would be upon raising incomes faster than prices rather than upon reducing the general price level. Nostalgia for a dollar of high value would have to be quenched by looking back to the last period in which it had a much higher value than now, the Great Depression of 1929-1939. The Almighty Dollar almost deserved the name then, considering the groceries and the servile politeness it could buy. But that dollar was mighty hard to come by for most people.

UNDERSTANDING INFLATION. Still another change in public thinking which would be necessary to make an all-go economy workable would be a clear distinction in the public mind between several kinds of inflation. The ordinary citizen would have to understand the difference between (1) expansionary inflation which would be part of an all-go economy; (2) runaway inflation which is a form of disaster; and (3) cost-push inflation which is depressing to the economy.

The mark of expansionary inflation is a gentle and beneficial rise of a great many desirable economic quantities—employment, output, prices, profits, wages, stock prices, incomes, savings, investments, the supply of money, and others. During an expansionary inflation, these values do not all rise by the same percentage, but they all rise in a relatively harmonious way, and the rise is gentle enough so that any rise beyond that which is necessary to maintain the all-go condition can be restrained by decelerating the anti-depression procedure.

Undesirable bubbles of speculation which may develop to mar the harmony—an excessive speculative boom in stock-market prices, for example, or sharp rises in the value of land which has been misrepresented to the public, can be dealt with by direct limitation of the flow of money to these areas.

Runaway inflation, sometimes called galloping inflation or hyperinflation, is something else. It is always caused by a pouring out of money from government printing presses.

Governments sometimes resort to huge printings of money because they want to spend large sums, but are unwilling or unable to raise any substantial part of the money by taxation or borrowing. Thus, the principal cases of runaway inflation are to be found when governments have really lost their power to govern and are desperately trying to stave off collapse. The runaway inflation in China before the Communists took over is a case in point. So much money was printed that pictures appeared in the newspapers showing a boy trundling a wheelbarrow full of paper money to the store to buy a piece of candy.

The fantastic inflation in Germany in the years 1919-1923 seems to have been related to political weakness, although the government survived. Incredible as it may seem, the price level in Germany rose by 150 billion times in those few years, based on issues of paper currency which by the end of 1923 totalled nearly 500 trillion marks. The value of the mark on the foreign exchange fell to a ratio of 42 billion marks to one United States cent. At the end of 1923, the Germans simply abolished the old currency and started using a new mark.

Such an inflation is highly disorganizing. At one stage in Germany in 1923, factory wages were paid twice a day and the wives of the workers waited at the gates each noon to seize the money and run off and spend it since it could become almost worthless in a few hours. In the department stores signs were suspended from the ceilings containing the amount by which the tag prices of goods were to be multiplied—one million, one hundred million, two hundred million and up. Meanwhile the government unfailingly printed more notes with more and more zeros behind the prime figures. Among other effects, very substantial shifts of wealth occurred in favor of debtors. The total mortgage debt of Germany, which in 1913 had been equal to one-sixth of the nation's wealth, was by 1923 not worth one American cent.[1]

Sometimes a runaway inflation will occur when a government is just getting established, but it is still from the same cause—large government expenditures paid for with huge amounts of paper money. The government of the United States issued such paper money to finance its war of independence against England, and there resulted the popular phrase "not worth a continental" to indicate anything as completely worthless as the individual continental came to be.

Runaway inflation has occurred in some developing economies, especially in Latin America, when governments have turned to the printing press to finance projects of national grandeur or projects of long-term development which will not for a long time put new goods and services at the disposal of consumers. The supply of goods and services has little flexibility in underdeveloped countries anyway, and the flood of printed money does not have to be enormous to start prices doubling or nearly doubling every year. And once the citizens see where the money is coming from, they fear for the value of all the money they possess. Then the rush is on to turn money into possessions at every opportunity, and this increase in the rapidity of spending money (what economists call the "velocity of circulation") adds to the inflationary pressure.

There is a third kind of inflation in addition to expansionary inflation and runaway inflation. It is called cost-push inflation. It begins with successful demands for higher wages of such magnitude that employers cannot offset them by improving their methods of production. This puts a squeeze upon the profits of businessmen and they react either by laying off some of their workers or by trying to pass on the higher costs to consumers in the form of higher prices. The consumers react in part by buying less of the higher-priced products, or, to the extent that they cannot conveniently do this, then partly by reducing their savings and partly by buying less of other things. The net effect is that more unemployment is caused in industry in general. As costs continue to rise and intensify the squeeze, unemployment will rise to the point at which workers will not have the power to continue the squeeze. It has been suggested that bankers might keep this kind of inflation going by extending easier credit to businessmen or consumers, but it is not clear that they would have a sensible motive for doing so in view of the poor prospects of the squeezed businessmen and the squeezed consumers.

It is important for the public not to confuse the wage increases which occur as a normal part of an expansionary inflation with those which cause a cost-push inflation. In an expansionary inflation, wages go up along with all other major economic quantities—employment, profits, prices, the stock market, etc. In a cost-push inflation, wages go up to such an extent that the other important quantities, except prices, decline. Employment declines, profits decline, the stock market falls, etc. During an expansionary inflation, it is all too common to hear some commentators castigating the rise in wages as causing a rise in the cost of living, whereas it is the rise in investment which is really driving the economy forward, with labor getting some of the benefit as the money goes around and around, and the ordinary citizen benefiting too as the rise in his income after taxes outstrips the rise in the cost of living.

For the sake of completeness we should also mention "administrative inflation" which results from the price-making power of a few large firms in certain industries. Thus prices of chemicals, aluminum, and autos, among others which could be cited, may rise more rapidly when prices in general are rising than they would if there were as much competition in those industries as in, say, the clothing industry.

Fortunately, administrative inflation usually has a "quality offset" which nullifies its disadvantages. This means that in the industries which have high price-power, there is also a higher than average rate of innovation leading to improvement in the quality of the product. The consumer may be paying a higher price than he would pay if these industries consisted of a larger number of smaller firms, but he is also getting a better product. It has been calculated that the average price of the "low-priced three" automobiles in the United States actually dropped 27 per cent from 1954 to 1960 if the cost of improvements over these years are counted in, although the index showed a rise in price of 34 per cent. To take another example, the cost of medical care in the United States rose by 30 per cent between 1957 and 1965, but as an offset, there was a large increase in the effectiveness of that care because of new drugs, new vaccines, new operative techniques, and new treatments for diseases such as cancer and polio.[2]

Administrative inflation, therefore, need not be a source of anxiety as long as the Schumpeterian correlation exists between price-power and quality-improvement.

Our understanding of the kinds of inflation has come so far that in future no one should use the word by itself. We should all say what we mean—whether expansionary, runaway, cost-push, or administrative inflation.

COMPENSATING THE VICTIMS. Another very substantial cost of an all-go economy would be reasonably just compensation for the victims of expansionary inflation. The public has become accustomed to the idea of at least partial compensation to the unemployed who are the principal victims of a policy of price stability. No such help has been arranged for the victims of the steadily rising cost-of-living which a higher rate of economic growth would bring. The reason for this neglect may lie partly in the diversity of groups put at a disadvantage by creeping inflation. An almost complete list would include the following:

1. Those living on old age pensions and old age insurance payments.
2. Those living on past savings or income from private insurance policies of fixed amounts.
3. The unemployed and unemployable whose payments from insurance and welfare usually do not rise as rapidly as prices.
4. Those living on receipts from debts—including mortgages, government bonds, and corporation bonds.
5. Teachers, civil servants, and other groups whose salaries are usually "sticky" in their response to higher costs of living.
6. Veterans and others living on disability compensation payments which usually do not rise as rapidly as prices in a full-employment economy.
7. Recipients of welfare payments—the blind, the sick, the old.
8. Those dependent upon the incomes of colleges, universities, hospitals, foundations, and some private corporations whose investments are restricted by law or custom to bonds of fixed value.

There are remedial measures to reduce the injustice these people would suffer in an all-go economy, just as the injustices of unemployment can be reduced in a go-stop economy. For example, all payments dependent upon legislative enactment can be automatically adjusted by law to changes in an index of the cost-of-living, in addition to whatever increases are thought desirable on other grounds. The face value of bonds, both private and public, can be similarly "indexed," with the advantage to the borrower that creditors will accept a lower rate of interest on bonds thus safeguarded. Indexed life insurance policies are already available from some insurance companies. The portfolios of universities, foundations, hospitals, and banks can be extended to include more securities whose values rise with the general level of prices. There is certainly an additional risk for such institutions in making a selection of such securities, but there is also a risk in keeping their money in so-called "safe" investments of fixed money value whose purchasing power is certain to deteriorate as expansionary inflation progresses.

Unfortunately, no one has figured out as yet what it would cost to do substantial justice to those hurt by inflation. The money devoted to this purpose would probably result in the attainment of full employment for the rest of the community somewhat sooner than otherwise. This assumes that the beneficiaries would spend the money more completely or more rapidly than those from whom it would be taken by taxation or any other method. It is probably safe to make this assumption since most of those who suffer from inflation, who could not themselves adapt their incomes to it, are in low-income groups.

Some commentators have suggested that doing justice to the victims of inflation would "add fuel to the fire" and drive an expansionary inflation into outright runaway inflation. This is not a credible argument since no expansionary inflation of record has ever become a runaway inflation. So long as the government does not resort to making money for its expenses by running the printing presses, a runaway inflation cannot result. An inflation of the expansionary type, resting upon increases in the supply of money based upon additional credit, public and private, wisely decided upon as a good investment, cannot run away. And it can always be slowed and even stopped, when wisdom so dictates, by running the anti-depression procedure in reverse for a while.

MORE UNBACKED MONEY. The fear of runaway inflation lies behind another public attitude that would have to be modified to make an all-go economy workable. That attitude prefers that money be made of something solid which has independent value, or be redeemable in some such solid thing, like gold or silver, or at least have a certain proportion of something solid behind it as a kind of ground anchor to keep the hyperinflationary balloon from going up.

This requirement has developed in the public mind out of a long memory of arbitrary increases in the supply of money made by unscrupulous kings to increase their own purchasing power at the expense of the value of their subjects' money. Even the great astronomer, Copernicus, took time away from his scientific studies to write a report to the Polish authorities protesting the practice by local princes of coin clipping—taking some of the metal from each coin as it passed through their hands and then melting down the clippings and recoining them. Copernicus pointed out that as the clipped coins circulated with the whole ones, people would hoard the whole ones and pass on the debased ones. Thus, he said (a few years before Gresham), bad money drives out good.

In modern economies the trend has been to lower the proportion of solid metal to the total amount of money, but to keep at least a minimum proportion so that the citizen can still feel that the volume of money is at least anchored to some solid object even though only a very small amount of his money is really backed by gold or silver and even less is actually redeemable in anything whose value he could test by the old-fashioned method of biting down on it.

In modern economies, also, the nature of money has changed so that most of what we use for money has no backing. Full-metalled coins have given way to tokens and to paper money, and paper money in turn has yielded place to bank deposits which are just ink marks on a card in a bank, and now are rapidly becoming just blips in a memory machine. Thus, in the United States, if we add up all the money people think they have—their checking accounts, their savings deposits, and their pocket money—we find the total in 1965 to be about 360 billion dollars. By contrast the gold held as monetary reserve by the federal government is about 12 billion dollars—or roughly 3 per cent of the total amount of money in the system. It is safe to say that hardly any resident of the United States considers that his money is adequately backed at three cents on the dollar.

Such a low backing disturbs very few economists, however, since the modern economic view is that the value of money is determined not by what is behind it but what is in front of it, in the form of goods and services for sale. To take an extreme case, if there is nothing for sale—no food, no housing, etc.—then money would have no real value in maintaining life even if it were fully redeemable in gold. And if the stores are amply stocked with things, then even the most unredeemable paper money will buy nourishment for human needs.

NEW INTERNATIONAL ARRANGEMENTS. Another cost of an all-go economy would be the necessity of co-ordinating the expansions of the several free nations by some kind of continuous international conference. An all-go economy is difficult for a single nation to accomplish alone if that nation depends substantially on foreign trade—and what nation does not in this interdependent world?

As one nation pursues full employment by expansionary policies while other nations are not in step with it, the expanding nation with its rising prices and costs soon runs into problems with its balance of payments with the outer world. If the nations are on the gold standard, gold will flow out from the expanding nation until it can no longer continue to play the gold standard game. If exchange rates between the several currencies are left free to fluctuate in relative values, then the currency of the expanding nation will be in ever greater supply and ever lower value in relation to the others.

To maintain an all-go economy, all the free nations should time their expansions to be in step with one another and adjust their relative rapidities of expansion to keep their international economic relations workable. This would require an international body of economists from each nation in practically continuous session, with a great deal of information at their fingertips and a great deal of respectful attention from national politicians and bankers.

One of the great values of such an international co-expansion policy would be the abolition of the kind of competitive depression in which great and supposedly sensible nations now engage. At this very writing, the dreary cycle has come round again and the major free nations are playing the old, sad game. Each one is trying to buy less from the others, to travel less abroad, to invest less in one another, to raise the highest barriers to others, to hold down its own wages and prices more than the others, and to abandon great enterprises of innovation and social justice lest they should increase prices inside the nation.

What are the objects of all this mutual mutilation? To try to export unemployment to other nations, to gain gold at their expense, to defend the existing price of each national currency in foreign markets. Under a system of international co-expansion, the nations could go forward together instead of backward in conflict and still keep the gold well distributed, the values of their currencies defended and unemployment at a minimum.

Summary

The most comforting thing about the issue of whether to rest content with a go-stop economy or to press on with the experiment of an all-go economy is that either course is so much more tolerable than the terrible alternatives so many nations faced only a generation ago between intolerable depression and intolerable dictatorship. Still, there are advantages and disadvantages in either course capable of arousing strong responses. Those who hate and fear unemployment, even at an average rate of only 5 per cent, point to the concentration of joblessness among the young, the unskilled, and the minority groups, and they cry shame upon society for not leaping into an all-go economy. Older heads reply with puritanic warnings: what goes up must come down; the higher you rise the harder you fall; the more you drink, the greater the hangover. Civilization, as Toynbee has said, is a movement upward, from plateau to plateau as climbers crawl up a mountain, resting at each newly-gained level place, wondering whether to try for a higher goal at the risk of falling to a lower one. What we have tried to do in this chapter, is to indicate the benefits and the costs of both policies in relation to full employment.

It is possible that the realities of political economy will produce a compromise which we might call the "mostly-go" economy which would have some expansionary inflation, but less than an all-go economy would require, and some permanent unemployment but less than a go-stop economy would require. It is safe to say that a mostly-go economy would be a broad target for both the expansionists and the stabilists.

CHAPTER 10

Taking It in Stride: the debt problem

The success of a free economy depends upon public understanding of its various parts and their functions. One of the most misunderstood parts of the system is debt, and if it continues to be misunderstood, there is serious danger that capitalism will not work nearly as well as it should. When we consider that total debt in the United States, public and private, now amounts to more than a trillion dollars, it is clear that we are dealing with no small matter.

A Matter of Morals?

Those who are against debt look upon it as unwise in particular and frightening in general. They are inclined to quote Shakespeare:

Neither a borrower nor a lender be
For loan oft loses both itself and friend,
And borrowing dulls the edge of husbandry.

And when they consider the future of nations, they tell us that growing debt will at worst bring national bankruptcy and at best put on posterity a cruel and hated burden. Such views, if carried into action would be depressive to a free economy.

To tackle Shakespeare first, let us remember that the little speech we have quoted was part of a larger admonition by Polonius to his son who was about to spend a year in sampling the pleasures of Paris, some of which, then as now, cost more than a young man's allowance was likely to cover. It is most doubtful whether this situation is on all fours with the debt problems of a national economy. To the economist, the kind of borrowing Shakespeare was referring to would be classified under the heading: "small interpersonal loans to the unemployed for purchases of non-durable consumers' goods and services; probable sub-group, wine, women and song."

In the national economy, the question that arises about debt is whether to use it to build factories and roads, to buy homes and farms, to construct dams for power and flood control, to buy arms, to finance preventive medicine, and to secure furniture, TV sets, college educations, and trips abroad for people who would have to wait much longer for such things if they had to be paid for in full at the time of purchase.

For the national economy, debt is, therefore, a tool for securing a certain result and not a moral issue. Like any other tool—fire or a steamroller—it has its uses, its limits, and its dangers.

Ratio Thinking Again

In relation to both national and personal debt, what is most important is for the public to become accustomed to thinking about ratios rather than about absolute quantities. Instead of staring with a single frightened eye at the trillion-dollar monolith of debt in the United States, the thinking citizen should open both eyes and widen his view to see the relation of that huge and growing debt to the huge and growing income and assets of the nation. For example, the value of annual production in the United States in 1966 will be about seven-tenths of a trillion dollars. If we suppose that by the end of that year total debt will be about 1.4 trillion dollars, then it is obvious that as a national economy our debt has a value equal to about two years' production.

Is that ratio too large? To find part of the answer to that question, we have to think of the assets which going into debt has enabled us to create. Debt enables an economy to have assets well in advance of the time when they could have been bought out of savings or taxes, and we have to consider whether the rate of interest we have to pay on the debt is too great a cost of having things now—both productive things and pleasurable things—rather than later.

Our minds might turn enviously to the American Indians who, as they rode over the Great Plains, were debt-free, and almost asset-free too. One wonders how great a consolation it was to them to bite the dust in a solvent condition while their conquerors were up to their coonskin caps in debt for the guns and ammunition and wagons and railways they used to clear the Indians from the plains.

Similar ratio thinking about the debt-asset relationship is essential if we are to have a perspective upon the burden of debt we hand down to future generations. The American Indians handed down no debt to their descendants of the present day, but they also handed down very few assets, as anyone visiting their reservations may observe. In considering our descendants, therefore, we must look not only at the debts we hand down to them but also at the equipment for production and pleasure we bequeath. If we must ask them to forgive us their debts, let us also remind them to appreciate the assets they have but didn't create themselves.

Alternatives to Debt

To understand debt we must consider the extent to which it is interchangeable with other quantities in the economy performing somewhat the same function. This requires us to look very broadly at the economy and at the place of debt in it.

Among several possible models of the whole economy, perhaps the most relevant for this purpose is the set of prosperity groups which we proposed in considering innovation as a component of capitalism. There we pictured our economic system as consisting of a series of groups of people, beginning with religious leaders and philosophers and going on through scientific theorists, researchers, inventors, investors, executives, employees, sellers, and consumers. It is down this chain of creation from stimuli through ideas, facts, models, investments, production, selling, and consumption that all the items comprising our prosperity have come and must in future come.

Where is debt in this picture? To find it we must put a magnifying glass on one group in the prosperity process—the investors. Looking closely at this group, we find that it is divided into two sub-groups, which we shall call the moneypoolers and the moneysprayers. (See Diagram III.)

The moneypoolers are the people who accumulate pools of money, not for the purpose of using it themselves, but rather to hand it over to others for productive use. Thus, among the moneypoolers we number the individuals who

DIAGRAM III
THE HANDOVER

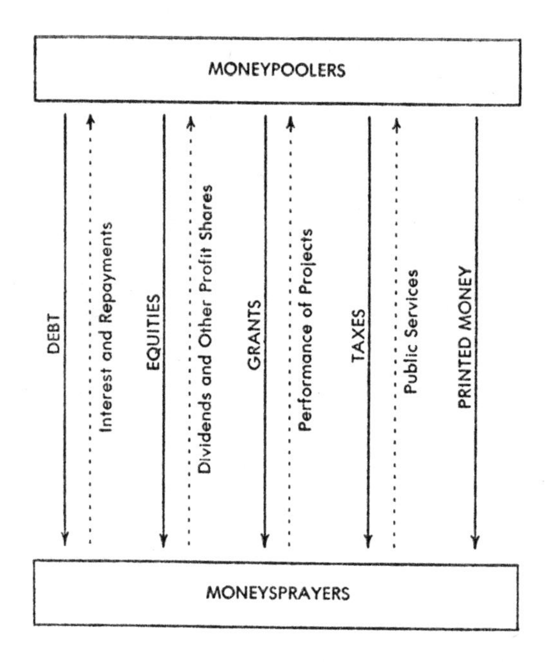

save, the insurance companies, the pension funds, the banks and other savings institutions, corporations which accumulate surpluses, and the taxpayers piling up their sums against the dreaded tax deadlines.

The moneysprayers are those who authorize the use of money in productive pursuits. They are the individual owners or partners in business, the boards of directors of corporations, the boards of trustees of colleges and hospitals, the congresses, parliaments, legislatures, county supervisors, and city councillors—whoever authorizes the planning of projects, contracts to get hold of the money, and appropriates funds to be spent. This group includes all who can spray money around the economy in definite patterns to attract land, labor, capital, and management for productive purposes.

The volume of money handed over by the moneypoolers to the moneysprayers in any period of time is absolutely vital to a prosperous economy. It determines the whole volume and direction of employment, including the rate of innovation, since it is the investors who determine what proportion of current production will be old inventions and what proportion will be new inventions.

Economists have not yet given a name to this total flow of productive funds between moneypoolers and moneysprayers. We propose to call it the *handover*.

The relevance of the handover to debt is that debt is one of the kinds of contracts under which moneypoolers hand over funds to moneysprayers. If the money passes between these two groups as a debt, then the contract has certain characteristics—the total sum is fixed, there is a date or dates of repayment, there is a rate of interest, and often there is a pledge of valuables in case of default.

But debt is not the only form of contract between moneypoolers and moneysprayers. There is also the kind of transaction called an equity. In that form, the pooler hands over his money to the sprayer in return for a promise that the sprayer will share his profits with the pooler if any profits are made and distributed. There is no promise of repayment, no rate of interest and no security. Investments in the stock market are of this type. So are investments by partners in their partnership, the reinvestment by corporations of their own surpluses in their own enterprises, and investment by individual businessmen in their own businesses.

A third form of transfer between poolers and sprayers is the grant. A grant is like a gift in that the grantor does not ask that the grantee ever return the money. However, there are usually other services asked in return. Grants are usually made by foundations, governments, and charitable groups for such purposes as research, education, and rehabilitation. Some corporations also make grants.

Taxes are another kind of transfer from pooler to sprayer. The government, as one moneysprayer among others, has sovereign power to oblige individuals and groups to pool money as tax dates approach and hand it over for public spending. So we must include taxes in addition to debts, equities, and grants as part of the total transfer from moneypoolers to moneysprayers.

Finally, there is a kind of transfer between moneypoolers and moneysprayers called "printed money." The possibility of this element in the handover arises from the right of most governments to create a supply of money. A government can accumulate a pool of money by coining metals, or by running the printing presses to print currency. The coinage of metals is so restricted by their limited supply and high cost that we need not give this source of pooling money much more than a passing glance. But paper and ink are cheap, and some governments resort to printed currency to bolster the amount of the total handover when they are unable to tax, borrow, or beg the amount they want by other means.

Modern governments in developed nations wisely rely very little upon such direct printing of currency, since governments in the past have exercised so little restraint once they got the presses rolling and have thereby brought on runaway inflations.

Modern governments do have in reserve and do sometimes use a device which is very much the same as printing money and which has disturbed many conservatives. In this process the government prints bonds and deposits them with the central bank of the nation (in the United States, the Federal Reserve System). In return, the central bank sets up a bank deposit in the government's name for the amount of the bonds and the government can then write checks on this amount. In short, the government has indirectly printed itself some money. Such indirect creation of money could be abused, but in a responsible democracy it does not appear to be a major danger, if kept for use in emergencies.

In sum, the total handover between moneypoolers and moneysprayers which drives the economy consists of several elements—debt, equities, grants, taxes, and printed money. Debt is an important part of this total driving force which has created all our income and all our production, and there is no sign that moneypoolers would willingly give up this form of contract with moneysprayers.

If we seek to reduce debt, therefore, we must be prepared to increase equally one or more of the other elements in the handover or else suffer a drop in money-pressure in the economy. Such a drop may be desirable if money-pressure is already too high for the level of employment desired, but it will be damaging if money-pressure is just adequate or less than adequate.

If we seek to change the debt-income ratio or the debt-asset ratio in the economy so that debt will be a smaller proportion, we have to take into account the fact that debt is usually a creator of income and assets. Reducing debt may in a particular case reduce income and assets by a greater proportion, thus creating an effect opposite to our intentions. Often the only way to improve these ratios is by increasing debt and using the proceeds so as to increase income and assets in greater proportion. This is not a matter upon which generalizations can be made for all cases. It takes a qualified expert to recommend in any particular case whether the way out of an unsatisfactory debt-income or debt-asset ratio is to increase or reduce debt.

In considering the function of debt in a free economy it is important to distinguish between pulsating debt and dead debt. Normal debt in a growing economy is pulsating, that is, money is borrowed by private or public groups and is put to work to build assets. As income accrues from these investments, the debt is paid off and new and larger sums are borrowed for greater expansion of assets. Thus the debt is continually paid off and renewed in larger amounts to keep the economy growing.

Dead debt is usually found in poor nations and sometimes in rich ones especially during depressions. It consists of debt which there is no longer much hope of paying off. It is a relic of vanished dreams and unsuccessful plans. The Bible records an ancient injunction to cancel outstanding debts every seven years, apparently in an effort to lift the burden of dead debt.

It is commonly observed that the peasantry in poor countries is terribly debt-ridden and in every village the frown of the moneylender is feared in the dusty streets. It is the moneylender who advances the money for seed and for the meager tools that hardly deserve the name, and for food to tide each family over between the empty bin and the next harvest. On the strength of these loans, the moneylender diverts to himself upwards of half the crop when it is gathered, and, as a result of foreclosures, he is likely to own about half the land, which he then lets out to the former owners as tenants. The peasant seldom gets out of debt to the village moneylender his whole life long and he wishes for freedom from debt as much as any freedom he can think of, and one might conclude that debt is a curse in these countries and that there should be less of it.

Yet the opposite is true. These peasants suffer from a

too-primitive system of debt. They should, as the farmers in prosperous countries do, command loans to consolidate larger farms, to buy adequate tools, to improve their soils and their crops, to educate their children and give them proper medical care, to store good crops against lean seasons. Much of this new debt would be long-term debt befitting the natural delay of return upon far-seeing investment. Proper lending agencies would not require the return of their money every year as the moneylenders do, and their rates of interest would be low, as in the prosperous countries. It is through a better debt-system, as one step among others, that the peasantry of the world can be freed of the fear and the burden of debt. More adequate credit to them is more likely to sharpen the edge of their husbandry than dull it.

In the prosperous nations, dangerous quantities of dead debt occur only during depressions and it is to be hoped that with the use of anti-depression procedures the last of such dangerous accumulations has occurred. Actually, it is only during depressions that total debt falls in developed nations. It falls because, as old debts are partly paid off, fewer prospectively profitable opportunities for investment present themselves and new loans decline in amount. The fewer new loans are made, the harder it is for people to get income to pay off old loans, and much of the existing debt may thus become dead. There are various devices for burying it—bankruptcies, liquidations, repudiations, moratoriums—but it is better not to let it occur. The best way to keep old debt from becoming dead is to create an adequate volume of new debt so that the income and assets necessary to pay off the old debt will come into being. Then the existing volume of debt will retain its important quality of pulsation.

Government Debt

Special fears and prejudices come into play when the ordinary citizen reasons about debt incurred by his government. The specter that haunts him most is called "national bankruptcy." Even economists are not immune from this fear; Adam Smith predicted that the government debts of his day would soon bankrupt the nations of Europe if they were not promptly reduced.

Speaking realistically, it is not easy to give substantial content to the term "national bankruptcy." What is it that would happen if a nation went bankrupt? We know what happens when a private business goes bankrupt. Usually the assets of the business are sold to private bidders, sometimes at auction, to satisfy at least part of the creditors' claims. Is this what would happen to the government of the United States if it went bankrupt? Would the White House go on the block, perhaps to be converted into a motel? Would the Pentagon be up for sale as a potential convention center? Could one perhaps pick up a national park for a song in this great distress sale? To ask these questions is to answer them. Bankruptcy in the usual business sense is not conceivable for a sovereign government.

Bankruptcy in private business is sometimes dealt with by appointing trustees to run the business for the benefit of the creditors until their proper claims are satisfied. Could this happen in Washington? Could the Supreme Court appoint men to take the place of Congressmen, the President, the Cabinet, and General Staff of the Armed Forces and instruct them to run the nation for the monetary benefit of the holders of government bonds upon which interest due had not been paid or whose principal had not been returned at date of maturity? Surely this would be unconstitutional in the United States and contrary to the sovereignty of any government.

There is no record of any nation having gone bankrupt in the business sense and it seems that the term "national bankruptcy" might as well be dropped from the language for lack of an ascertainable meaning. Governments have fallen, have been overthrown, have been removed from office by adverse elections, have had their powers shorn and in other ways have incurred disadvantages and displeasures, sometimes from failing to pay their debts, but they have not gone bankrupt.

Actually governments can feel safer about going into debt than private businesses because governments have the right to tax their creditors to help pay what they owe the creditors, and they can also tax the beneficiaries of their spending to recover some of the money for the purpose of paying interest and principal on loans. The ordinary businessman or consumer would feel himself lucky indeed if he could levy upon the bank which loaned him the money to help him pay the bank, or if he had the power to tax the persons upon whom he spent the money to help him pay off his debts.

It has often been said that governments, whatever their powers, should be careful about going into debt, in order to avoid passing on the burden of it to future generations. We are sometimes asked to pity the American infant in his cradle, shackled at birth by so great weight of public debt around his little neck that he must scarcely be able to raise his head. Indeed, why should he raise it, since he has no more cheerful prospect in life than to plod along under this burden until he in turn has to fasten it around the necks of his own babies? This fear fails to take account of an immense fact; although the total public debt of a nation, per capita, is an impressive figure, this figure is very much higher in prosperous nations than in poor ones. So one must not neglect to mention, along with the public debt each infant inherits, the assets he also inherits. Usually the higher the debt figure, the higher the national wealth which the child will have as part of his environment in life. A nation without public debt is almost always a nation without development.

Still another fear arises from the fact that interest payments must be made on public debt. We sometimes hear that these payments, rising ever higher on a rising debt, must some day swallow up all our income. It is true that when $100 of new debt is incurred, and spent in the community, the community must eventually repay, say, $105 in principal plus interest. However, this will be difficult only if, at the time of repayment, the circulation of money has not risen by that extra amount, and this in turn will happen only if debt (or some other element of the handover) has not increased meanwhile. Interest payments become a burden only if debt (or other elements of the handover between moneypoolers and moneysprayers) does not increase rapidly enough. This accounts for the fact that interest is hardest to pay and most often defaulted during depressions when total debt is decreasing. This decrease reduces money-pressure, which gives people less income from which to pay the interest. Thus, interest payments on public debt as a percentage of the annual Gross National Product reached the highest level in the history of the United States during the 1930's when depression was deepest! But taken over the long run they have not increased at all. On the debt of the United States government alone, interest charges were 2 per cent of the Gross National Product in 1868 and less than 2 per cent in 1965, although the debt had risen more than 100 times. There is simply no basis in experience or logic for the fear that rising total debt leads to an interest burden increasingly difficult to pay. On the contrary, it is only when debt and other components of the handover fail to rise rapidly enough to create the income and assets required for prosperity that interest payments become a rising percentage of national income.

The public fear of public debt is magnified also by what we might call "the red illusion," that is, the impression that the government is running at a loss in every year in which the budget is not balanced. The public knows that no private business could run indefinitely "in the red" and fears for the fate of the government. However, the government uses an accounting device which no private businessman in his right mind would use; it figures investment expenditures each year as though they were operating expenses.

When a private firm is doing so well that it borrows money to build a new plant, it does not record the investment in the operating expense column for that year and tell its stockholders that it is losing money. It has instead an investment budget separate from its operating budget. The government needs to adopt the businessman's practice in this respect to avoid creating the illusion that it is operating at an unproductive loss when in fact it is creating valuable assets for the future.

The problem of the red illusion is complicated by the fact that government can afford to take the profit from a public enterprise in a wider variety of ways than a private business could afford. A private business must usually see a direct and identifiable money profit from its operations within a predictable period after the costs are incurred. The government, with its borrowing and taxing powers, can afford to wait longer for its profit, or simply let expenditure go into general circulation without attempting any direct recovery of costs, expecting instead to tax the general circulation of money at various points to recover the money. The government also has the option of accepting an expenditure as an asset to the community without ever trying to recover its cost. In that case there will be a permanent increase in public debt to balance the estimated value of the asset.

In pursuance of this special latitude, governments have made investments which would have shown up as a loss on private books, but which are generally admitted to have been sound investments. The construction of the Canadian National Railway by the Canadian government is often cited as an example. So is the Louisiana Purchase by which the United States government acquired the Mississippi Valley. Public health programs are often put in this category. Perhaps the greatest of such expenditures is the winning of wars against foreign aggressors. How could we compare the profit of such an expenditure against its cost?

Once we have cleared from our minds unnecessary fears and illusions about public debt, we can move on to form a philosophy of such debt based upon the part which public investment should play in a free economy.

One way to begin thinking about the desirable extent of public investment in a free economy is to look at its role in each of the components of capitalism.

1. *Competition*. It is clear that the government has a part to play in bringing as many citizens as possible to a condition of competitive capability by the time they leave school and enter upon the workaday world. This means developing each person's health, skill, motivation, mobility, general knowledge, and spirit of independence to the point where each one will be an economic man or woman in the classical sense. Most of the public investment for this purpose will be in education, supplemented by investment in public health and some subsidies to housing. We might call this public investment the "pre-competitive" sector.

2. *Innovation*. It seems desirable to have some public investment in the earlier stages of this component—those in

which scientific theorists and scientific researchers work, and even some subsidy to invention. It is a paradox of our prosperity that it depends so firmly upon science, and yet scientists, especially basic theorists and pioneering research workers, find it difficult to secure funds for support and equipment. When Einstein was working out his formulas for atomic energy, he could not even get a job teaching school and had to resort to clerical work in a patent office. The more advanced the research, the farther in the future will any profitable application of it occur, and perhaps the more helpful it is likely to be when it comes. But private enterprise is not sufficiently hospitable to these long-term projects, and public investment in them is required if the rate of innovation is to be at its best. We might call this "pre-innovative" public investment.

3. *The anti-depression procedure.* This requires some public investment in the central bank and its regional auxiliaries. But most of all it requires the timing of public investments so that they are heavier when private investment falls off and lighter when private investment is highly active. It is not always advisable, however, to advance or postpone government expenditures to fit into an anti-depression pattern, and it may be wiser to rely upon changes in taxation to achieve quickly the desired effect. Thus there is an "anti-depression" category of desirable public investment.

4. *Countervailing power.* Public investment is required for legislative investigation and for regulatory agencies to be sure that the power of the several organized groups is kept in reasonable balance. The theory of countervailing power also includes the concepts of balanced investment and a balanced supply of consumers' goods, and the achievement of these balances will certainly involve the government in expenditures. Balance in the supply of physi-

cal capital, for example, means construction of roads, ports, airfields, dams, urban rapid transit, and other physical works without which private physical capital would be much less effective. Balance in the supply of consumers' goods requires public money to be spent for parks, playing fields, marinas, beaches, music centers, libraries, museums, and other cultural and recreational facilities.

5. *Stimulation.* It would seem that this is mainly a function of the family and of the religious institutions of society. Some stimulation might be accomplished through public investment in the schools, but in the developed nations there is a tendency toward separation of religious and ethical teaching from the public school system. There is also a tendency to separate the family from the public school and to have the school take over more responsibility for children at an earlier age. This may result in a lessening of stimulation unless the schools see the need to increase their contribution to it and invent ways to stimulate students which do not conflict with constitutional restrictions upon religious and ethical teachings.

Since at least four of the five components of capitalism require a measure of government investment for their proper functioning, the outlook is toward an ever-increasing government debt as the nation's economy grows. There seems to be no practicable way to avoid this and no special reason to fear it if the government money is spent for needed and useful projects.

It would be theoretically possible to increase taxes by enough to pay for most new public investment but taxes are already very high and very irritating to most citizens, and it might be dangerous politically to try to escape increases in public debt in this way. There are those who see superior morality in paying for improvements as they are built, so that once in operation they are debt free, but to the economist it seems equally moral to pay for improvements as we use them. Assets are easier to finance on the pay-as-you-use principle.

A permanently rising public debt will thus have to be accepted by the public as one more thing that goes up in a growing free economy. The citizen's consolation will have to come from ratio thinking and from his growing wealth in public assets.

There is probably no escaping the label of "socialism" for the public segment of a free economy. Yet it is worth noting that modern public investment has a different character from public investment recommended by socialists. The socialist idea is to replace private investment with public investment as a matter of principle because, in their opinion, capitalism is unfair, inefficient, and evil. Modern public investment in a free economy, however, is substantially co-operative, supportive, and complementary to private investment. The roads, ports, dams, laboratories, scholarships, hospitals, and parks financed by government in a free economy contain no socialist presumption that private investment is undesirable. On the contrary, under capitalism, one of the objects of greater public investment is to lay the groundwork for greater private investment.

Foreign Debt

Another specific kind of debt that arouses special fears is money borrowed from people in other nations. It is said that money we borrow within the United States is money we owe to ourselves, whereas borrowing abroad means that we will be losing something of value when we pay interest and repay the principal.

Here again, the only way to correct the false view is by ratio thinking. Borrowing abroad is usually done to create assets here and these assets usually increase our production and our ability to make payments to the creditors. We need therefore to compare the increase in our ability to earn money abroad with the increase in our need to pay money abroad, both resulting from the debt.

There is usually a special reason for borrowing abroad. Perhaps the rate of interest and the terms of repayment are more favorable. Perhaps the money is obtainable from foreigners when it is not available at all from domestic sources. These facts create another ratio—the costs of borrowing abroad in comparison with the costs of borrowing the same amount in our own country. The advantages offered by foreign creditors may clearly offset the difficulty, if any, which we expect to encounter in making the payments to them.

On the whole, the record of the results of foreign borrowing is excellent. The great economic expansion of the United States from pre-Revolutionary days until World War I was substantially financed by British capital. And British capital also financed a major part of economic development in India, Africa, and South America. Since World War II, capital from the United States has financed important projects in a great many countries. The fact is that underdeveloped nations are not able to raise much capital within themselves, and their choice is usually not between domestic capital and foreign capital, but between much foreign capital and very little domestic capital.

Where foreign debt has brought trouble, it has usually been for lack of adequate countervailing power between domestic borrower and foreign creditor. Sometimes the foreign creditors have been so strong that they could use military force to take over the borrowing country. In other cases, the creditors have been able to control the borrowing nation by economic threats.

These forms of imperialism have become highly unacceptable in the modern world. Unfortunately, they have been replaced by the opposite extreme, an irresponsible and damaging excess of power in the hands of borrowing countries. Regularly in recent years, borrowing nations have simply taken over foreign properties and assets, usually with dubious plans for compensation. How these borrower nations expect to attract needed foreign capital in the future is a mystery.

What the world economy very much needs is a code of foreign capital, embodied in a standard treaty recognized by international authority, which will apply to all foreign lending and borrowing. Such a code should rule out all the evil manifestations of old-time imperialism on the part of the creditors and all the new-style confiscations, partial or complete, on the part of the borrowers. The immediate purpose should be to free the borrowers from fear of domination and the creditors from fear of being financially wiped out. The ultimate purpose should be to increase very greatly the flow of funds across national boundaries. When we compare the distribution of available capital in the world with the distribution of poverty, it is obvious that an ample flow of foreign investment is an absolutely necessary link in the chain of development.

Underdeveloped nations which doubt the workability of any such arrangement should study the borrowing relationships between Great Britain and the United States from 1790 to 1920. The United States was careful to achieve during its Revolution only political independence from Great Britain so that it would have the countervailing power to continue to get ample British capital without submitting to imperialism. In return it gave security to British capital so that it need not fear any kind of confiscation.

Consumer Debt

Consumer debt is probably the most feared of all by social commentators. And debt is in fact a dangerous tool in the hands of the individual family if it is not properly handled. Some families do not have sufficient want-control to prevent overdebt, and it is safe to say that every low-income and middle-income family should have a professional, independent debt-counselor just as they should have a family physician or medical group. One hopes for a rapid development of this new profession of debt-counselling. Many families get into debt-trouble because of unexpected disability of the breadwinner, and it is heartening to see that so many debt-contracts now provide insurance, at some extra cost, to pay off the debt without burdening the family in which catastrophe has struck. Similar insurance could also take care of families caught by natural disasters.

The laws of personal bankruptcy in many states also permit a family to escape overdebt and still retain enough assets to carry on as a unit, but a careful professional watch needs to be kept on the operation of these laws to prevent corrupt practices.

On the positive side, one great advantage of consumer debt is that it allows people to enjoy goods and services much earlier in life than if they had to save up the whole price before buying. Perhaps nothing is more astonishing to foreign visitors to the United States than the quality of housing, transportation, household appliances, education, and entertainment which young families can enjoy by going into debt. To some, it may seem immoral to have the use of so many things so young, but to an economist there is nothing wrong in the pay-as-you-use principle.

From the point of view of the whole economy, one value of consumer debt is its expansionary effect. There is a saying that "one man's debt is another man's income," and it is true that the existence of millions of consumers who are qualified to be in debt and who know how to handle it can be greatly stimulating to employment. In such an economy, the income which each family has with which to pay off its debt depends substantially upon other families going into debt. The whole volume of consumer debt thus does not become a danger so long as new debt (or other elements of the handover) is being created at a sufficient rate.

Consumer debt, therefore, is a quantity that is likely to increase indefinitely in a growing economy, and consolation, if desired, must be sought in ratio thinking about the rise in incomes and assets which go with it.

Conclusion

The problem of unnecessary fears and worries about debt could be met semantically by replacing the word "debt" with the word "credit." The total volume of debt in an economy is, of course, precisely the total volume of credit. But it sounds much less fearsome to speak of consumer credit and the national credit rather than consumer debt or national debt. We do this already when we speak of credit unions instead of calling them debt unions. It sounds so much more acceptable to say that in a growing economy the volume of credit, both private and public, must be expected to increase indefinitely than it does to say the same thing about debt, although the statements are the same.

In this chapter we have chosen to meet the problem head on and make our case with the dreaded name itself. Debt is a tool in the economy, not a moral issue. It is a tool for creating income and productive capital. Debt is one form of the handover between moneypoolers and moneysprayers and needs to be reasoned about in the light of the other four forms—equities, grants, taxes, and printed money. An adequate total handover is essential to our production, employment, and income.

We have found no reason to be especially afraid of public debt, foreign debt, or consumer debt. They all have their special advantages and dangers.

What is important for the public is not to focus attention upon debt alone, but to think of its ratios to income, production, employment, and assets and to think of it as a driving force in creating these benefits. Like other forces, it needs watching and calls for sensible controls, but its growth is more to be favored than feared in a free economy.

Part III

The Struggle for the World

CHAPTER **11**

Can Man Help Himself?— Marxism and other determinisms

The economic theory which we have been presenting says that a successful free economy depends upon the making of choices which are substantially right concerning all of the necessary components of the system by nearly all of the people involved in the economy. There is nothing inevitable about the rightness of the choices nor about their completeness. Success may be partial in any degree and the whole range from success to failure is available to all human groups.

The main opposition to our theory is the idea that economic progress is determined by factors beyond man's control. There are a number of such theories, and in this chapter we shall try to show why they are not valid, because the economic future of man depends first of all upon his ridding his mind of deterministic discouragements.

Some of these theories say that the pattern of economic growth is determined by outside physical forces—climate, trade routes, natural resources, or natural drift. There are other theories that make economic development depend upon the presence of certain humans—a certain race, or certain heroes. And, finally, there are the "ballet" type theories, saying that man proceeds on his road between poverty and prosperity by pre-determined steps which he cannot change. In this group we shall discuss the theories of Brooks Adams, Oswald Spengler, and Karl Marx.

Climate and Drift

The search for simplicity in economic thinking led first to the idea that climate is the determining factor in economic development. The English historian, Henry Buckle, wrote a three-volume treatise called *The History of Civilization in England* (1869) just to prove this. Among the intelligentsia of the late nineteenth century, it was as much a mark of sophistication to have read Buckle (or at least to have his volumes in the bookcase) as it is today to have read *The Affluent Society*. Buckle said that climate does its work on economic development through psychology. Where the happenings of Nature are huge and violent—storms, earthquakes, searing suns, vast tracts of ice and snow—man is intimidated and he responds by producing great quantities of art, literature, religious belief, and superstitious myth rather than economic progress. But where the look of Nature is gentle and kindly, man grows confident and develops an analytical mind which leads him on to scientific discoveries and prosperity. Only in Europe, Buckle concluded, was Nature benign enough to make prosperity possible.

Unfortunately for Buckle's theory, we now have prosperity not only in Europe but on the hot plains of Texas and amid the ice and snow of Minnesota, as well as in the least "benign" climates of Europe, which include Switzerland, Norway, Sweden, and Finland. If climate were really the main factor determining economic development, we should expect to see on our world map two bands of prosperity circling the globe in the temperate zones, one in the northern and the other in the southern hemisphere. In fact, the temperate zones show little development where they cross Asia, Africa, and South America. And even in Europe there are extreme variations of prosperity and poverty within the zone of "benign" climate.

Speaking historically, the centers of economic development have changed location frequently in the past 4000 years, and this has posed serious problems for "climate" theorists. To try to reconcile fact and theory, several hypotheses have been formulated postulating a "drift" either of development or of climate. Thus we read of the "equatorial drift" of civilization in R. Decourcy Ward's *Climate Considered Especially in Relation to Man* (1918). In the opposite direction, we read of "The Coldward Course of Progress" in an article by S. C. Gilfillan in the *Political Science Quarterly* (1920).

And not to neglect a third point of the compass, we recall Bishop Berkeley's melodious words:

> Westward the course of empire takes its way:
> Time's noblest offspring is the last.

Of all the drift theories, this one contains the most comfort for the undeveloped nations since, by the bounty of Providence, every place is west of everywhere else in the round world. If prosperity continues to drift westward, sooner or later everyone's turn will come, not only to be prosperous, but also to be noble!—at least for a while, until history staggers on.

Actually, history has staggered along the path of economic development. The earliest known centers of a substantial degree of prosperity, relative, of course, to their times, were several cities in India. After they declined, prosperity went westward into Asia Minor, then south to Egypt and eastward to China, then west again to Greece and again west to Rome, then in succession, east to Byzantium, south to the Moslem empire, north to Italy (in the Renaissance), west to Spain, and on north through France and the Low Countries. At about the same time, there was the great westward movement of prosperity to North America and the south-and-eastward movement to Australia and New Zealand, and the westward movement to Japan.

It seems, therefore, that there are no uniformities of economic development patterned after changes in climate, even when the concept of "drift" of one sort or another is brought in. There is no regular pattern of drift either.

Even if we suppose, with Professor Ellsworth Huntington of Yale, that the temperate zones themselves have drifted widely in historical time, as he indicates in his *Mainsprings of Civilization* (1945), there is still no close correlation with the tides of prosperity and poverty. Climate has been one of the problems some human groups have struggled to overcome, and often they have succeeded by the grace of will and technique. Thus the simplest of all causative theories of development (and simplicity is a great virtue, though not the only virtue of a good theory) has had to be abandoned.

Natural Resources

Determinism has also been sought in another simple theory that would have us believe that natural resources determine the pattern of economic development. If this were strictly true, then we would expect a global map of development to correspond to a global map of resources. Such is obviously not the case. Huge areas of undeveloped resources lie in Latin America, in India, in central Asia, and probably in Africa, in areas where people are among the poorest in the world. And in other areas weak in resources, people are prosperous. England has no oil; Japan no oil or iron; Switzerland has nothing in the way of basic resources; Holland, Belgium and Denmark have almost nothing. The patterns of resources and development simply do not correspond.

The fact is that some human groups weak in resources have gone out and acquired supplies of them. Certainly, as world trade is organized today, no nation need be poor because it lacks basic materials in its own earth.

One peculiarity of natural resources is that they have always been natural, but usually they have become resources only as the result of human steps toward prosperity. Iron was not a resource until people wanted to build machinery and tall buildings. Oil was not a resource until the internal-combustion engine came into general use. Uranium was only a waste-product of mining, sometimes useful for coloring glass, until the atomic engine was invented. Even the immense resources of the United States in land itself were not really usable until the settlers from Europe applied to them the steam railroad and farm machinery. The American Indians found the vastness of the Great Plains a hindrance and left the rich soil almost unmarked by cultivation or mining.

Experience indicates that a nation which has a will to prosperity is likely to find upon its own ground, and beneath it, unexpected means. Switzerland was late in discovering the value of its scenery for tourism. Greece, with scenery just as fine and with classical ruins in addition, has been even later, and is only now awakening to provide facilities for the tourism that can help ease the pain of its poverty. The Dutch discovered that the watery wastes of their territory could be converted into fertile fields. And the Venetians found that a beautiful city could be built on piles sunk in shallow seas. In short, resourcefulness can often make resources.

Sometimes an attempt is made to save the natural-resource theory of economic development by linking it with trade routes, saying that resources are valuable only when they are close to such routes and that development occurs along the major routes. It is easy to understand the appeal of such a theory, since a prosperous nation, such as England in the nineteenth century, was surely the center of the economic world, as the United States is today, and as Rome was long ago when all roads led there.

But support for this theory comes only from observing the world as it is at any one time. It cannot stand the test of history. History shows us that nearly every nation which has stood prosperously in the center of things began its climb to prosperity from a place on the edge of the existing economic world. It rose by its own efforts, the efforts of its prosperity-minded groups, to become a center of economic life. Rome started as a hill town on the edge of the empire of Greece, and drew the Mediterranean world around itself like a cloak. England, too, began her rise from the position of an island fortress beyond the northwestern brink of a Europe in which Spain was the center of traffic between the Old World and the New. And Spain itself had been for centuries an outpost of the Roman Empire and then, for more centuries a province of the Moslem empire, before it decided to become a center of economic life. With regard to the United States, it is hardly necessary to say that its present central position was built by its own efforts from a wilderness which originally was several thousand miles west of everywhere of importance.

Prosperity therefore does not depend upon being near major trade routes or near accessible centers of comfortable wealth. The seeds of new prosperities have more often been germinated in remote provinces and on difficult frontiers.

Schoolchildren are often told by their textbooks that the earliest centers of prosperity occurred thousands of years ago in fertile river valleys and deltas because the environment there was favorable to a certain ease of living. The rivers usually mentioned are the Nile, the Tigris, the Euphrates, and the Yellow River in China. But, as Toynbee reminds us, these fluvial environments could not have been "the cause" of the prosperity, since most such river valleys in the world produced no advanced degree of civilization. Toynbee mentions the Jordan, the Indus, the Ganges, the Yangtze, the Mississippi, the Rio Grande, the Colorado, the Congo, the Amazon, and the Danube as having produced no early economic development. So the river theory, like the other environmental determinisms of economic development, is not supported by the evidence.

Races

Another form of deterministic thinking links economic growth to the presence of certain kinds of human beings—say a certain race or certain strong men.

Theories that only one race of people is capable of prosperity, or entitled to it, are still vivid in the minds of living persons who helped defeat the German and Japanese ideas of racial superiority during World War II. And in many of the new nations there are lively memories of theories of Anglo-Saxon racial superiority. Cecil Rhodes, the English multimillionaire who held a virtual monopoly of the world's supply of diamonds, wrote in his *Confession of Faith* (1877):

> I contend that we are the finest race in the world and that the more of the world that we inhabit the better it is for the human race. Just fancy those parts that are inhabited by the most despicable specimens of human beings, what an alteration there would be in them if they were brought under Anglo-Saxon influence.[1]

Rhodes provided in his will that all of his vast fortune should go to the support of a society to extend British rule and British colonies to the parts of the world he thought they were entitled to, i.e.,

> the entire Continent of Africa, the Holy Land, the valley of the Euphrates, the islands of Cyprus and Candia, the whole of South America, the islands of the Pacific not heretofore possessed by Great Britain, the whole of the Malay archipelago, the seaboard of China and Japan, and the ultimate recovery of the United States of America as an integral part of the British Empire.[2]

Fortunately for his ultimate reputation, Rhodes changed his will before he died, deleting the empire-seeking society and providing instead for scholarships at Oxford. His example shows, however, how tenacious a hold racial theories have in the human mind that they can arise even at high levels of civilized societies.

It is a curious coincidence that the authors of racial-superiority theories have always nominated for superiority the very race to which they themselves belonged. The world has yet to see a racial theorist who proclaims the superiority of another race than his own.

Another form of racism calls for the removal of a certain race of people as a necessary condition of prosperity. The principal victims of this deterministic idea have been the Jews, and in modern times the major anti-Jewish theorist has been Karl Marx.

In his essays *The Jewish Question* and *The Capacity of Today's Jews and Christians to Become Free* (now published together under the title *A World Without Jews* [1959]), Marx says that the Jews are the root of all evil in the world since they are the source of the worship of usury and money as God. He writes: "What is the object of the Jew's worship in this world? Usury. What is his worldly God? Money." [3]

His conclusion develops promptly: "Very well then: emancipation from usury and money, that is from practical, real Judaism, would constitute the emancipation of our time." [4]

According to Marx, the evil capitalist spirit among Christians is the result of their spiritual conquest by the Jews. "Christianity sprang from Judaism; it has now dissolved itself back into Judaism. The Christian was from the start the theorizing Jew; the Jew, therefore, the practical Christian; and the practical Christian has once more become Jew." [5]

This conquest was necessary to the Jews, Marx writes, because: "Only then could Jewry become universally dominant and turn alienated man and alienated nature into alienable, salable objects, subject to the serfdom of egotistical needs and to usury." [6]

Marx propagated the idea that the Jew rules the world through a conspiracy of money power. "The Jew who is, for example, merely tolerated in Vienna determines by his money power the fate of the entire German Empire. The Jew, who is without rights in the smallest German state, decides the fate of Europe." [7]

There seems to have been no doubt in Marx's mind that there were evil results of Jewish influence. He writes:

> What is stated as theory in Jewish religion, namely contempt for theory, art, history and man as an end in himself, is an actual and conscious point of view held to be virtuous by the man of money. Even the relations between man and woman become an object of commerce. The woman is auctioned off.[8]

Thus Marx made a distinction between other religions which he said were opiates of the people designed to keep them tranquil under capitalist exploitation and the Jewish religion and race which he regarded as the active corrupting agent of mankind.

The rise of the people of the United States to the highest standards of living has refuted most racist doctrines, since the American population is so great a mixture of races and nationalities. An anthropologist has suggested that when a citizen of the United States says fervently, "I thank God that I am a 100 per cent American," he must reflect that the word "thank" comes from German and Scandinavian sources by way of England, that God was originally the deity of the Hebrews, that the number 100 arises from the invention of the zero by the Arabs, that "per cent" refers to a decimal system created by the Greeks, and that the word "American" itself comes from the name of an Italian geographer.

Historically, no one race has been uniformly prosperous at any one time. World economic leadership has changed from race to race. For the first fifteen centuries of the Christian era, the flow of science and invention was all from China to the West. We remember how astonished Marco Polo was at the standard of living in Cathay. And for several centuries, roughly from the ninth to the twelfth centuries A.D., the Arabic peoples of the Moslem empire led the whole world in every branch of prosperity. The economic rise of the whitest race inhabiting and spreading out from Europe has come only in the past five centuries, beginning with the Spanish and Italian explorations of the world geographically and in science and art during the Renaissance. Thus racism must be judged an unproductive theory in accounting for economic development.

Heroes

A deterministic theory even more widely held than racism is the "hero" theory, the idea that prosperity for any nation must await the coming of a "strong man," a "man on horseback" who will know what has to be done to create prosperity and will knock heads together to force people to do it. Thomas Carlyle was a great emphasizer of the role of heroes in human affairs. And the philosopher, Nietzsche, seemed to be recommending the leadership of society by huge, cruel, and exultant heroes.

An enormous amount of time is wasted in every poor nation of the world in waiting for such a hero, in debating whether this man or that is the awaited leader, in hailing a new hero or in disgracing an old one.

There are two kinds of these heroes. One kind promises to bring prosperity by unifying lands that have been divided. He will create a "Greater Co-Prosperity Sphere" of some sort, as Hitler proposed to do in Europe and the Emperor of Japan in Asia just a few years ago. The other kind promises to divide what has been united, to secure freedom from alien rule, to remove foreign restrictions, and release native energies.

Sometimes the heroes unify or divide as they have promised, but they find invariably that neither unity nor division is sufficient for prosperity. To make prosperity where there was poverty requires a change in the poor individuals themselves—in their state of mind, in their skills, and in their group relationships, along with all the other procedures for prosperity we have described in the preceding chapters. Heroic dictators have a very poor record of achievement in these fields, and when they have disappointed the hopes of their followers, they usually lead them on to some disaster.

If the hero is of the unifying type, he is likely to try to compensate for failure by taking refuge in greater unifications, to be achieved usually by war, and he asks his own people to sacrifice more and to postpone their hopes for prosperity until this or that greater unification is achieved.

If the hero is of the divisive type, he is likely to meet the disappointed hopes of his people by imposing an iron dictatorship upon them, rewarding a powerful few with great prizes and enslaving the rest of the population. What he should do is simply to resign his rule while admitting that the task of creating prosperity is plainly beyond him, but one seldom encounters this reaction among dictators.

The tragedy is that so many hundreds of millions of people in the world are still waiting for the nostrum of heroic leadership to ease their lot by some political magic. In his shortest poem, William Butler Yeats, a great friend of Irish freedom from British rule, expressed this thought in connection with a leader of the Irish Rebellion:

> Parnell came down the road, he said to a cheering man:
> 'Ireland shall get her freedom and you still break stone.'

It is very much worth noting that the most prosperous nations of the world today do not show patterns of economic growth highly correlated with degrees of heroic leadership. These nations have taken the surer way of building all the components of capitalism and spreading its opportunities to ever larger sections of the population. If these things are done as a part of an almost universal understanding of the requirements of a free economy, the hero becomes superfluous and the alternating terrors and tediums of dictatorship need not be borne.

Fixed Dances: Spengler, Adams, and Marx

There is yet another class of economic determinisms which we call fixed-dance theories because they say that mankind must go through certain specified stages in economic growth, as though engaged in a huge and unalterable ballet. Some of these ballets are cyclical in that they see humanity as going through endlessly repeated performances of good and evil without the sense or the power to change the script. Other such "ballet" theories predict straight-line dances to some predestined end.

The most famous cyclical theory is that of Oswald Spengler. In *The Decline of the West* (1917), he insists that civilizations are organisms with a determined life cycle of rise and fall:

> Civilizations are organisms, and world history is their collective biography. The immense history of the Chinese or of the Classical civilization is the exact equivalent of the petty history of the individual man or of the animal or the tree or the flower.[9]

When we ask how such an "organism" comes into being, Spengler tells us that:

> A civilization is born in the moment when a great soul awakens out of the proto-spirituality of ever-childish humanity and detaches itself, a form from the formless, a bounded and mortal thing from the boundless and enduring. It blooms on the soil of an exactly definable landscape to which, like a plant, it remains bound. It dies when this soul has actualized the full sum of its possibilities in the shape of peoples, languages, dogmas, arts, states and services, and reverts into the proto-soul.[10]

Such a theory is disappointing to economists for two reasons. The first is that it is impossible to disprove. What goes on in the high, clouded realms where "great souls" are conceived in "proto-spirituality" is beyond our ken and seems likely to remain so. It is like the theory that storms are caused by the anger of the gods. To refute it we should have to show that during particular storms all of the gods felt happy, a task of rare difficulty.

The second reason for our disappointment with Spengler's theory is that it seems to dash our hopes for a very general human prosperity. The appearance now and then and here and there of islands of prosperity in a sea of "ever-childish" humanity does not meet our ambitions. We need some way to call down the necessary spirituality everywhere.

It is somewhat surprising to find that the only American to forge in his mind a theory of economic growth and decline has given us a cyclical theory. Brooks Adams, brother of the more famous Henry Adams, wrote in *The Law of Civilization and Decay* (1896), that prosperity wherever it is found in the world begins with an invasion of a settled civilization by barbarian hordes and ends in the same way.

According to Adams, the barbarian invasion shocks the society into a state of fear and this induces it to select leaders who can cope with fear—military leaders to reduce it, religious leaders to console it, artistic leaders to sublimate it, ideas of chivalry and romantic love to sweeten it. In Europe after the fall of Rome, there was such a period which we call the Middle Ages.

Then, Adams says, as the economy achieves stability, its chief motive shifts from fear to greed, and it selects its leaders from the business world. At first it is the producers (the manufacturers) who lead, and later it is the sellers (the merchants). But as the economy becomes ever more greedy, moneymaking becomes an end in itself and the financiers come to the top.

The financiers concentrate more and more power into their own hands, according to Adams, by ingeniously and fiendishly causing a series of prosperities and depressions. They create periods of prosperity by opening their hoards of money to enterprising borrowers who want to produce goods and services. Then when new assets have been created, the financiers tighten credit, cause a depression, and take over another large slice of the economy by foreclosure. By repeating this process, the financiers concentrate more and more of the wealth into their own hands while the worker is forced to sell his labor for less and less. Finally, when there is no more for the financiers to take over, the economy stagnates, and decay sets in until there is a new infusion of barbarian blood.

The tragedy of modern times, according to Adams, is that we have reached stagnation and there are no barbarians left to reinvigorate us into a new period of fear!

The reader acquainted with Marx will recognize a strong similarity between his theory and Adams'. The principal difference is that Marxism is not cyclical. Instead, it sets up, for free economies, a straight-line series of increasing evils leading to revolution, dictatorship, and a communist utopia. The twelve stations on this Marxian road to ruin and redemption are as follows:

1. *The materialistic view of history.* Marx wrote that the economic basis of a society determines all its other characteristics. He said that if he knew how a human group made its living he could derive from that its government, its culture, its amusements, its social structure, and everything else, as Sherlock Holmes might reconstruct a man's build from his footprint. Consequently, said Marx, whatever

change is made in society has to begin with some change in its economic methods.

2. *The class struggle.* Marx thought that the main instrument of change in human affairs was the struggle of the lower classes to get the upper classes out of the saddle. The struggles of slaves against masters, of serfs against lords, of workers against industrialists are the dynamos of history. On many occasions, Marx said, these struggles have been blind revolts without plan or future, but he saw his role as that of giving the masses a purpose for revolution and the blueprint of a perfect society.

3. *The labor theory of value.* Marx said that the only value in any good or service is the labor that goes into it. Consequently, in his view, anyone other than a laborer who shares in the proceeds is an exploiter and a parasite. The economists of the nineteenth century were saying at the same time that the production of anything requires four things: land, labor, capital, and enterprise, and they called these the "factors of production." It followed from their reasoning that the owners of all four factors—the landlords, the workers, the bondholders and stockholders, and the managers—were all entitled to a share of the revenue of the business. Marx denied this, and set the goal of the newest class struggle as the elimination of receipts by any group except the workers.

4. *Increasing monopoly in industry.* It was Marx's prediction that economic power under capitalism would gravitate ever more completely to the big monopolists, squeezing the small businessmen down into the working class.

5. *The increasing misery of the working classes.* Marx said that under capitalism the receipts of the non-worker groups would increase because of the monopoly of power in their hands, and the standard of living of the workers would become increasingly lower.

6. *The increasing severity of depressions.* Marx predicted that deeper, longer, and more frequent depressions would shock the capitalist system as the "monopoly capitalists" arrogated to themselves more and more of the purchasing power.

7. *The increasing reserve army of the unemployed.* As depressions increased, Marx said, more and more of the workers would become more or less permanently unemployed. This, he predicted, would be welcomed and encouraged by the capitalists, because the sight of so many of their fellow workers out of work would intimidate the employed workers and restrain their demands for a living wage.

8. *Imperialism and war as delaying the ultimate revolt of the workers.* Marxists say that the capitalist nations might delay the Communist revolution temporarily, and even provide their own workers with a temporary rise in their condition of life, by conquering and harnessing the natives of the underdeveloped countries. The revolutionary energies of the workers could also be diverted for a time by involving their emotions in nationalistic wars.

9. *The inevitability of world revolution.* Ultimately, according to Marx, the workers will see that nothing but world revolution can help them, and this revolution, peaceful if possible, violent if necessary, will, he says, take place under Communist leadership.

10. *The dictatorship of the proletariat.* Marx foresaw in his theory a period after the revolution when the workers would live under a dictatorship of their own leaders. This dictatorial period would last as long as capitalistic elements existed, either as groups of persons or as the persistence of capitalistic memories and thoughts within the individual.

11. *The abolition of classes.* When all thoughts of capitalism and free enterprise had disappeared from humanity,

then, Marx said, distinctions of rich and poor would vanish, and each person would be willing to produce according to his ability and receive according to his need. The abolition of classes would make this utopia permanent, since the struggle of classes with one another has been the only dynamo of historical change.

12. *The withering away of the state.* Government, Marx promised, will no longer be necessary in the new utopia, since every person will from his own internal convictions be a selfless contributor to the group. The restraints and penalties imposed by government will therefore not be required, and the state will wither and die, leaving the new Marxist men and women to enjoy their paradise in freedom.

Marx's theory, like the other deterministic ones, denies any human ability to see when human affairs are going badly and to change them for the better. Marx utterly failed to see that humanity can, in free societies, get together to correct evil tendencies. In fact, every one of the "inevitable evils" of capitalism which he foresaw has been substantially remedied in the more prosperous nations of the world. The wealthy classes in those nations do not consist of oppressive parasites, but of men and women who, for the most part, make their contribution to the welfare of the world and regard their wealth as substantially held in stewardship for the world. The working classes in those nations have not become increasingly miserable, but enjoy a rising standard of living, and this is not obtained by exploiting colonial peoples. On the contrary, billions of dollars in aid are being sent every year from the richer nations to the poorer. Depressions have not become increasingly severe nor unemployment progressively higher under capitalism because anti-depression procedures have been set up to prevent these evils. Monopoly has not increased its relative strength because countervailing powers have been developed against this. Consequently, the whole Marxian prescription of destructive revolution, dictatorial purgatory and the eventual utopia of "new Marxist Man" becomes unnecessary and would be grossly destructive to human progress.

Conclusion

In summary, the position which economic thought has now reached is that there is no deterministic factor which bars any human group from a lasting prosperity in a free society. The limiting factor is the will of the people themselves, and this is most strongly conditioned by their religion or philosophy of life.

History has shown us examples of prosperity made of apparently most unpromising materials. Toynbee notes that the ancient Greeks, finding themselves upon a rocky, difficult peninsula in the Mediterranean, one of the hardest places on earth to make a living, nevertheless made one. They discovered that the olive tree and the grapevine would grow in the sparse soil. They found clay and set up workshops to make earthenware to contain the olive oil and the wine. They built merchant ships to carry these products abroad. And they found silver and dug it up to be molded into money to finance all this. The results in terms of philosophy, art, and empire are among the brightest pages in history.

There is no reason to suppose that Greece is an isolated example. As Toynbee remarks, if one sets out to mark upon a map the three places in Europe where prosperity would be least probable, one's pencil could easily fall upon the once flooded plains of the North Sea Coast where Holland is, the landlocked, once all but impassable mountains which are now Switzerland, and the shallow, marshy seas where Venice stands.

Intellectually, therefore, economic determinism is dead. But we are not sure that it will be buried. It may be embalmed and covered with gold and worshipped as a god. Its image may be printed on flags and carried into battle. Its appeal may hypnotize whole nations into making armed tours of other people's territory. Poets may declare it as W. H. Auden did when he wrote:

> From the narrow window of my fourth-floor room
> I smoke into the night, and watch reflections
> Stretch in the harbour. In the houses
> The little pianos are closed, and a clock strikes.
> And all sway forward on the dangerous flood
> Of history, that never sleeps or dies,
> And, held one moment, burns the hand.[11]

Free people know that they can make the necessary tools to grasp history and turn it to the advantage of mankind.

CHAPTER **12**

Which System Will Win?— the chances of capitalism

In the great battle of economic ideologies for possession of the human mind, capitalism is at a disadvantage on several counts. For one thing, its very lack of determinism works against it. It contains no rigid doctrine that it is the only goal toward which all history has been moving with perfect compulsion, or that it is the gateway to a heaven on earth. These are Communist claims.

All that capitalism can say is that it is an experimental try at a higher stage in human evolution, the synthesis of prosperity with freedom. We cannot claim with certainty that all the world's people will be capable of meeting the conditions of the synthesis, although there is no apparent reason why any human group should fail if it is willing to make all the kinds of effort needed.

Nor can capitalism say that people who achieve it can relax in utopia. Combining prosperity and freedom requires the maintenance of a number of components and the continual solution of a number of problems in an arena of human frailties and human pressures, and a great deal can and does and always will go wrong in these areas from time to time. Eternal vigilance and eternal learning and even eternal change are the price of successful capitalism.

Capitalism suffers also from the disadvantage of having been built up gradually from imperfect beginnings which involved a great deal of suffering and some close brushes with total disaster. Only after the hardest kind of trial and error have its essential components been added one by one to meet slowly recognized needs. Meanwhile, the memory of incomplete forms of capitalism and their persistence in parts of the capitalist world today remain in the minds of men and in the propaganda of dictatorships.

Capitalism also has the handicap that it calls for the participation of nearly every human being in its continual process of choices. In its complete form capitalism is inevitably linked with political democracy, with its continuous peaceful reconsideration of choices, and with its peaceful changes in social direction. To the hardy believer in the long-run human adventure, this is one of its greatest assets, but those who are wary of the weaknesses of ordinary human nature grow pale at the prospect of putting so great a reliance upon it.

Capitalism's Future in the Developed Nations

With regard to the developed capitalist nations, a degree of confidence seems justified about their capacity to go on building the components of capitalism and operating the system.

In relation to the component of competition, most of these nations are strengthening the abilities of their people to be economic men and women in the classical sense. In the United States there seems now to be a determination to carry this kind of investment into even the poorest and most alienated groups of the population under the banner of an anti-poverty program.

With respect to the component of innovation, there is a growing appreciation in the developed nations of the necessity of strengthening it all along the line, especially in the earlier stages of scientific theory and scientific research.

The United States is fortunate also that, among the groups in the middle of the innovative process, the agreements between labor unions and managements do not restrict innovation (except in certain special crafts). It is most important that this freedom of management to innovate be preserved, while, at the same time, the employees be guarded by good wages and special plans to prevent them from excessive loss of income when innovation forces them to move out of their jobs and readjust their activities.

And we should note that at the end of the innovative process, consumers are beginning to insist that new products be of good design, reliable in performance, and honestly advertised. They are also beginning to demand that poisonous and ugly by-products of innovation be prevented so that the affluent society will not become the "effluent" society as well.

In the matter of the third component of capitalism, the anti-depression procedure, good progress is being made among the developed nations in learning when and how to use it. By operating it relentlessly, the nations of western Europe have been able to keep unemployment at a negative figure for years at a time while they import hundreds of thousands of workers from southern Europe and North

Africa. In England and the United States, the procedure has been used to maintain a good average level of employment on a go-stop basis, with mild recessions alternating with bursts of nearly full employment. As more and more conservatives understand the necessity of this component to the success of capitalism, we may expect its operation to be more prompt in heading off recessions.

As for countervailing power, the fourth component of capitalism, we see that progressing also in the developed nations. Organization into economic groups is being pressed even among the poor, the unemployed, the aged, college students, teachers, and consumers, in an attempt to achieve the fully organized society. And new laws and practices are coming into being to regulate the relations between organizations and their members in an effort to eliminate the tyranny, corruption, and secrecy which could ruin many of the benefits of a countervailed society.

One further advance that is certain to come in this component is more discussion and research on the question of when power is adequately countervailed. What are the signals that one group is too powerful and another not powerful enough?

As for the final component of capitalism, stimulation, we find in the developed nations a complex picture. The decline in religious teaching in the schools, and the loss of some of the teaching functions of the family suggest that the newer generation may be less motivated to economic advancement than their forefathers.

At the same time, the progress of automation suggests that some drop in stimulation may be in order somewhere in the system, provided that non-destructive uses of leisure can be found.

Overstimulation is apparent in some families whose members struggle vainly to achieve a measure of contentment in the face of wants which always rise faster than their incomes. This whole segment of society needs a degree of want-control, whether it be achieved by chemical tranquilizers, philosophies such as Zen, Yoga, and Tao imported from understimulated countries, or just plain thinking about the meaning of life.

All in all, the outlook for capitalism in the developed nations seems favorable. Communism which has so often boasted that it would overtake and pass the standard of living in capitalist nations is now seen to be dropping back, steadily or unsteadily, and to be increasingly dependent upon the capitalist nations even for food. The outlook is that only a small minority of voters in capitalist nations will see any sense in the idea of imposing communism upon their successful economies.

Thus capitalism now has no important ideological rivals in the developed nations, unless we count as such the possibility of fascism. But fascism, like communism, has been so deeply discredited as a workable economic system that its revival seems unlikely.

This century has seen fascism take two forms—the blustering militarism and genocidal massacres of Hitler and the quietism of weaker fascist nations. This second kind of fascism still exists in some nations and offers a spurious stability. There is one dictator, one doctrine, and one loyalty, and no ordinary citizen need bother his head about politics or economics. If he does, he is likely to be shot or shut away. Under this quietism, the social order of rich and poor, of aristocrat and commoner, is determined from above, and the burden of self-improvement is lifted from the shoulders of the people. Innovation is discouraged, with the result that there are a great many old buildings and old ways and the easy laughter and sad songs of the poor for foreign tourists to enjoy.

But quietist fascism is now threatened with upheaval in the Latin and African and Asiatic nations where it is still in power. The time bomb of increasing population ticks for them too, and if it brings an actual impoverishment of the already low fascist standard of living, then the people will begin to heed the foreign tourists, the foreign soldiers on local bases, and the foreign radio broadcasts which bring them tidings of a freer and more prosperous life under democratic capitalism.

The Way Forward from Communism and Fascism

When the nations now under dictatorships do undertake to combine freedom and prosperity, it will be important that they be provided with guidelines for making the transition. Unfortunately this part of economic theory is completely undeveloped. It is of great urgency that economists and other social scientists do the necessary thinking and research.

Recent experiments in Russia with the profit motive, consumer-oriented production plans, and partially free markets for a few goods in a few places have led some observers to the conclusion that the Soviet economy may have already begun the journey toward a free society. But these changes may be only the swing of the pendulum, which all dictatorial organizations show, between centralization and decentralization. While they are at one extreme, its difficulties become increasingly obvious and the virtues of the other extreme more attractive. After a change to the opposite condition, the same process takes place and the pendulum swings again. But whether the pendulum is moving toward centralization or decentralization, the system remains a dictatorship. Whatever freedom is allowed today in a dictatorship can be revoked tomorrow, or even late this afternoon.

A true sign of a turn toward capitalism in the Communist countries would be the granting of individual rights which could not be taken away by the State. The Soviet economy would first have to come forward as far as Magna Carta and then work its way along as quickly as possible to the Bill of Rights of the Constitution of the United States.

Freedom of enterprise would have to come next, that is, the freedom of an individual or group to employ others under the procedures of countervailing power, which guard most employment in the Western nations from the exploitations criticized by Marx.

Upon these foundations, the Communist nations could gradually build up the components of a free economy as the democracies have done, not forgetting that political democracy is an essential companion of successful capitalism.

The return of a nation from fascism would be easier in some ways than the return from communism, since fascist governments, when they have come to power, have not murdered or exiled the investing and owning classes as the communists did. These skills of private investment and ownership would have to be built up from zero in a Communist state, but in a fascist state the present owners and investors would only have to get used to other groups countervailing their power and to being more innovative themselves.

The Prospects in the Underdeveloped Nations

The development of free and prosperous economies has the same requirements in poor nations as in rich ones. There is not one theory of economic development for the rich and another for the poor. The same components of capitalism have to be built up and the same major problems coped with in Asia and Africa as in Sweden and New Zealand.

The poor nations will have less trouble with some problems, automation for example, and more with others, such as population, but apart from differences in emphasis the theory of capitalist development is the same for all parts of the world.

What distinguishes the poor nations is that they are nearer the beginning of the developmental process and at the same time have fewer resources to spare from the daily struggle for existence with which to promote development. These nations seem also to have less zest for the long climb ahead, less heart for the sacrifices it will require, and more hope that some miracle of divine favor or foreign aid or conquest of traditional enemies will do it for them.

In every underdeveloped nation there are many rich and powerful men from whom strong leadership in development might be expected, but they too seem so often to be content to play and sleep in well-upholstered comfort, disregarding the rough wooden boxes of dynamite under the polished floors of their mansions. The ingredients of the dynamite are well known to social chemists. The explosive consists of one part population increase, one part rising expectations of a better standard of living, and one part the means to violence supplied by revolutionary communism. Thus far economists have not been able to prescribe a method of defusing this mixture so that economic development can go forward in orderly and peaceful ways.

The outlook in most of the underdeveloped nations, therefore, is for a period, perhaps decades long, during which matters will get worse rather than better. The rate of population increase is already greatest in the countries which can least afford it, and it seems almost certain that at least some of them will be faced with a period of mass starvation before they achieve numbers control and enough productivity to reverse the present trend.

No one can contemplate starvation on any scale with equanimity, but it will seem especially cruel for any part of the human race to have to go through a period of it just when ordinary people the world over have been led to expect substantial improvements in living conditions in their own lifetimes. It is unfortunate that so much publicity about foreign aid and the Peace Corps and the work of private charities in poor countries has helped to raise such hopes by its failure to point out the elementary arithmetic of these endeavors. Foreign aid from the United States since World War II has totalled more than a hundred billion dollars, but this has amounted to only two dollars per year per person in the receiving nations. This is good as far as it goes, but it will not, no matter how wisely concentrated or distributed, make the difference between poverty and a satisfactory standard of living. Much of it, of course, has been invested in methods to save and prolong lives, a project impeccable in virtue, but a project whose success intensifies the problem of food.

Thus foreign aid at its present level and as it is now administered cannot be depended upon to stem the tide of economic deterioration in the underdeveloped nations. The same is true of personal services such as are rendered by members of the Peace Corps and by workers sent from churches and charitable foundations. While they are teaching one slum-dweller to read, a dozen others are growing up illiterate, and while they are teaching one peasant how to cultivate his land, his wife bears more children than the land can support. The charitable efforts are good in themselves, but they do not and cannot, as now organized, reverse the course of the disease of poverty.

The world's best hope is that there will be a Great Awakening in the underdeveloped nations to the fact that they will probably have to do at least 90 per cent of the development job themselves, and that they must have the determination to build the components of a free economy, even if it takes a hundred years or more, and to meet the operating problems of the system competently, even under unfavorable pressures of excess population, false hopes, and threats of dictatorship.

The underdeveloped nations cannot rely upon being swept along by any tide in the affairs of men toward a more prosperous world or by any natural tendency in the world economy to bring the standard of living in poor nations closer to that of the rich. In his book, *Rich Lands and Poor* (1957), Gunnar Myrdal has shown that there is actually an opposite tendency for rich nations to get richer and poor nations poorer in the absence of immense efforts to the contrary. Observing that such figures as are available show that about two-thirds of the world's population now has a real income per head less than their ancestors had a century ago, Myrdal says this shows the operation of an old American saying, "Them as has, gits." It is even true, he says, within the poor nations themselves where the contrasts between rich and poor are growing greater.

These considerations do not warrant an ultimate pessimism, but they do indicate that the underdeveloped nations face a long struggle and that they should not be discouraged by the length of time required. Dr. W. W. Rostow notes in *The Stages of Economic Growth* (1960) that each of the developed nations took about sixty years to reach industrial maturity after they seriously began to try for it. It is not likely therefore that a presently underdeveloped nation could reasonably expect an advanced economic development in less than a century.

At this moment in history, the most difficulty in attaining a complete capitalism in underdeveloped nations apart from population troubles seems to be experienced with the component of countervailing power. Attempts to keep one group or another in control of each nation in the old-fashioned way by a series of rebellions, revolutions, coups, countercoups, interventions, massacres, and executions put off the day of economic progress and damage the existing economic structure. A way has to be found to convince the rulers of those nations that relief from this series of disasters lies in organizing a government of the people in which each person is represented through his groups as well as through his individual rights and his vote.

The foundation of countervailing power is, of course, the organized group—the industry, the labor union, the teachers' association, the scientists' federation, the government bureau, and all the rest. These groups themselves are often unformed in poor nations, and a primary task is to build them from the ground up in community after community until a government based on countervailing power is feasible.

The live-and-let-live philosophy of countervailing power must also be accepted. No group must aim at absolute power. No powerful group must be allowed to exile or execute or silence the others. The arbitration of minor disputes must be arranged. When these and the other principles of countervailing power are part of the life of a nation, then it will have changing governments within a stable political system and it can go forward with the other components of capitalism.

In the realm of innovation there are also immense tasks in the underdeveloped nations. The rich must be made productive and innovative and the poor must accept a realistic schedule for the satisfaction of their hopes. This is especially true of the ancient hope of nearly every rural family to have a farm of its own and to feel the security of land ownership. In view of the coming food crisis, humanity cannot afford to handle its land in that way until the "numbers hump" has been passed. There may come a time when basic foods will be synthetically produced and then the land can be devoted to decoration, recreation, and the raising of tasty seasonings and natural supplements to the basic foods, but between now and then it is a matter of life and death that land be scientifically managed in large units so that each farm family grows enough to feed not only itself but many other families as well. Obviously this will mean a change in the present practices of land management in the poor nations.

In the matter of full employment, most economists agree that there is a great deal of concealed unemployment in the poor nations, especially on the land. Many rural workers put in a full day's work only sporadically. No economist would object to such unemployment as a pleasant variation from the intensity of life as observed in the developed nations, but where the need is as great as it is in the undeveloped nations, survival requires a change.

Perhaps the greatest challenge to the poorer nations lies in the area of stimulation. They need a complete and conscious Prosperity Ethic developed from reformations of their own traditions and beliefs. One result of such a new ethic should be the elimination of the pervasive graft, bribery, and corruption in official circles that now waste so much of nearly every productive effort in these nations.

One advantage the less developed nations may have is a choice of whether to commit their efforts to imitating all the urban complexities of life in the present prosperous nations or whether to try to develop simpler alternatives which will give them substantial comfort and freedom without the problems of crowding, tension, and pollution of presently prosperous cities. The people of the poorer nations may be impressed with the desire so many prosperous people show to spend their weekends, vacations, and retired years in simpler environments.

Conclusion

In sum, there is qualified good hope that the experiment various nations have embarked upon since 1776 of trying to combine prosperity and freedom will succeed and will become worldwide. There is the population hump to be gotten over in the coming decades, and there is destructive militarism to be suppressed, and there is an understanding of the components and problems of a complete capitalism to be made part of nearly everyone's mind and will. That is as far as we can see ahead, or need to see right now.

Notes to Chapters

CHAPTER 2

1. Alfred Marshall, *Principles of Economics* (Eighth Edition; London: Macmillan and Company, 1920), pp. 717-718.
2. T. R. Malthus, *An Essay on the Principle of Population* (Second Edition; London: J. Johnson, 1803), p. vii.
3. T. R. Malthus, *Principles of Political Economy* (Second Edition 1836; New York: Augustus M. Kelly, Inc., 1951), p. 226.
4. *Ibid.*, p. 226.
5. *Ibid.*, pp. 226-227.
6. Charles Darwin, *The Origin of Species and The Descent of Man* (New York: The Modern Library), p. 490.
7. *Ibid.*, p. 509.
8. *Ibid.*, p. 504.
9. *Ibid.*, p. 508.
10. *Ibid.*, p. 498.
11. *Ibid.*, pp. 498-500.

CHAPTER 3

1. *Capitalism, Socialism and Democracy* (Second Edition; New York: Harper & Brothers, 1947), p. 82.
2. *Ibid.*, pp. 137-138.

CHAPTER 4

1. (London: Macmillan and Company, Limited, 1936), p. 379. The British Commonwealth rights to use quotations from John Maynard Keynes, *The General Theory of Employment, Interest and Money* have been granted by courtesy of Macmillan and Company, Limited, and the Trustees of the Estate of the late Lord Keynes. American rights granted by the U.S. publisher, Harcourt, Brace & World, Inc.
2. *Ibid.*, p. 307.
3. *Ibid.*, p. 245.
4. (New York: Oxford University Press, 1954), p. 280.
5. Keynes, *op. cit.*, p. 159.
6. *Ibid.*, p. 374.
7. *Ibid.*, p. 374.

CHAPTER 5

1. *The Economics of Collective Action* (New York: The Macmillan Company, 1951), p. 28.
2. *Ibid.*, p. 141.
3. *Ibid.*, p. 22.
4. *The Affluent Society* (Boston: The Houghton Mifflin Company, 1958), p. 252.
5. (New York: The Macmillan Company, 1924), p. 79.
6. P. 149.
7. (Boston: The Houghton Mifflin Company, 1956), p. 152.
8. P. 23.
9. *Ibid.*, p. 283.
10. *American Capitalism*, p. 152.
11. (New York: The Macmillan Company, 1934), pp. 72-73.
12. *Myself*, pp. 155-157.
13. *Ibid.*, p. 159.
14. *The Economics of Collective Action*, p. 23.
15. *Ibid.*, pp. 34-35.
16. *Myself*, p. 143.

CHAPTER 6

1. *Luther's Epistle Sermons*, translated by John Nicholas Lenkers (Minneapolis: The Luther Press, 1909), Vol. II, pp. 280-281.
2. *Works of Martin Luther* (Philadelphia: A. J. Holman Co. and The Castle Press, 1915), Vol. I, p. 279.
3. *Luther's Epistle Sermons, op. cit.*, Vol. II, p. 278.
4. *Works of Martin Luther* (Philadelphia: A. J. Holman Co. and The Castle Press, 1931), Vol. IV, pp. 14-15.
5. *Ibid.*, p. 224.

6. *Works of Martin Luther* (Philadelphia: Muhlenberg Press, 1915), Vol. II, p. 161.
7. *Ibid.*, p. 160.
8. (Philadelphia: Presbyterian Board of Christian Education, 1936), Vol. I, p. 757.
9. *Ibid.*, pp. 761-762.
10. *Ibid.*, p. 597.
11. *Ibid.*, Vol. II, p. 787.
12. *Ibid.*, Vol. I, p. 791.
13. Sir Abdullah al-Mamum al-Sahrawardy, *The Sayings of Muhammad*, with foreword by Mahatma Gandhi (London: John Murray, 1954).
14. Majid Fakhry, *Islamic Occasionalism* (London: George Allen and Unwin, Ltd., 1958), pp. 14-15, 56-82.
15. Gamal Nasser, *Egypt's Liberation—The Philosophy of the Revolution* (Washington, D.C.: Public Affairs Press, 1955), pp. 112-113.
16. Floyd H. Ross, *The Meaning of Life in Hinduism and Buddhism* (Boston: The Beacon Press, 1952), pp. 13-19.
17. *Ibid.*, p. 87.
18. *Ibid.*, p. 44.
19. Albert Schweitzer, *Out of My Life and Thought* (Mentor Book Edition; New York: Henry Holt and Company, 1953), p. 119.
20. Ross, *op. cit.*, p. 68.
21. *Ibid.*, p. 77.
22. Sarvepalli Radhakrishnan, *Eastern Religions and Western Thought* (Second Edition; London: Oxford University Press, 1940), pp. 352-354.
23. *Ibid.*, p. 353.
24. Ross, *op. cit.*, p. 35.
25. *Ibid.*, p. 73.
26. Radhakrishnan, *op. cit.*, p. 27.

27. *Ibid.*, p. 31.
28. *Ibid.*, p. 85.
29. *Ibid.*, p. 86.
30. *Ibid.*, pp. 85, 89, 94, 95.
31. *Ibid.*, pp. 371-373.
32. *Ibid.*, pp. 357-364.
33. *Ibid.*, pp. 367-368.
34. Quoted in D. C. Holtom, *Modern Japan and Shinto Nationalism* (Chicago: The University of Chicago Press, 1943), p. 6.
35. William K. Bunce, *Religions in Japan* (Rutland, Vermont: Charles E. Tuttle Company, 1955), p. 167.
36. *Ibid.*, pp. 167-169.
37. Kishimoto Hideo, Editor, *Japanese Religion in the Meiji Era*, translated and adapted by John F. Howes (Tokyo: Obunsha, 1956), p. 21.

CHAPTER 7

1. Edward H. Graham, *Natural Principles of Land Use* (New York: Oxford University Press, 1944), p. 61.
2. W. C. Allee, Alfred E. Emerson, Orlando Park, Karl L. Schmidt, *Principles of Animal Ecology* (Philadelphia and London: W. B. Saunders Company, 1949), p. 428.
3. *Ibid.*, p. 701.
4. Wendell G. Swank, "Nesting and Production of the Mourning Doves in Texas," *Ecology*, Vol. 36 (1955), p. 500.
5. F. S. Bodenheimer, *Problems of Animal Ecology* (New York: Oxford University Press, 1938), p. 135.
6. K. Myers and W. E. Poole, "A Study of the Biology of the Wild Rabbit in Confined Populations," *The Journal of Ecology*, Vol. 51 (1963), p. 450.

7. Robert L. Strecker and John T. Emlen, Jr., "Regulatory Mechanisms in House-Mouse Populations: The Effect of Food Supply on a Confined Population," *Ecology*, Vol. 34 (1953), pp. 375-385.
8. Robert L. Strecker, "Regulatory Mechanisms in House-Mouse Populations: The Effect of Limited Food Supply on an Unconfined Population," *Ecology*, Vol. 35 (1954), pp. 249-253.
9. Charles H. Southwick, "The Population Dynamics of Confined House-Mice Supplied with Unlimited Food," *Ecology*, Vol. 36 (1955), pp. 212-225.
10. Shelby D. Gerking, "Evidence for the Concept of Home Range and Territory in Stream Fishes," *Ecology*, Vol. 34 (1953), pp. 347-365.
11. Bernard S. Martof, "Territoriality in the Green Frog," *Ecology*, Vol. 34 (1953), pp. 165-174.
12. Allee, *et al.*, *op. cit.*, p. 236.
13. *Ibid.*, p. 598.

CHAPTER 8

1. J. M. Keynes, "My Early Beliefs," in *Essays and Sketches in Biography* (New York: Meridian Books, 1956).
   Roy Harrod, *The Life of John Maynard Keynes* (New York: St. Martin's Press, 1963).
   Leonard Woolf, *Sowing* (London: Hogarth Press, 1960), and *Growing* (London: Hogarth Press, 1961).

CHAPTER 9

1. For a general account of this German experience, see Frank D. Graham, *Exchange, Prices and Production in Hyper-Inflation Germany, 1920-1923* (Princeton: Princeton University Press, 1930).
2. Richard Ruggles, "The Problems of Our Price Indexes," in *The Battle Against Unemployment*, edited by Arthur M. Okun (New York: W. W. Norton Company, Inc., 1965).

CHAPTER 11

1. Quoted by Frank Aydelotte in *The American Rhodes Scholarships* (Princeton, New Jersey: Princeton University Press, 1946), p. 4.
2. *Ibid.*, p. 5.
3. Karl Marx, *A World Without Jews,* translated from the original German with an Introduction by Dagobert D. Runes (New York: The Philosophical Library, 1959), p. 37.
4. *Ibid.*, p. 37.
5. *Ibid.*, p. 43.
6. *Ibid.*, p. 44.
7. *Ibid.*, p. 38.
8. *Ibid.*, p. 42.
9. Oswald Spengler, *The Decline of the West* (New York: Alfred A. Knopf, 1939), p. 104.
10. *Ibid.*, p. 106.
11. From Poem XXX of *On This Island* (Second Edition; New York: Random House, 1937), p. 66.